Dyslexia
Included

Dyslexia Included

A Whole School Approach

Edited by
Michael Thomson

David Fulton Publishers
London

David Fulton Publishers Ltd
The Chiswick Centre, 414 Chiswick High Road, London W4 5TF

www.fultonpublishers.co.uk

David Fulton Publishers is a division of Granada Learning Ltd, part of the Granada Media Group.

First published 2003
10 9 8 7 6 5 4 3 2 1

British Library Cataloguing in Publication Data
A catalogue record for this book is available from the British Library.

ISBN 1 84312 002 X

Typeset by BookEns Ltd, Royston, Hertfordshire
Printed and bound in Great Britain by Thanet Press Limited, Margate, Kent

Contents

The contributors

All of the contributors have been involved in conference presentation and courses that we run for parents and teachers at East Court.

Anne Bailey

Anne teaches General Studies, but also helps with specialist English, so her role is in accessing the curriculum for our pupils. Anne is a graduate in History and Education, has a PGCE and has been at East Court since 1999.

Tom Broughton

Tom is responsible for ICT teaching and management as well as teaching Mathematics and has overseen the computer networking of the school. He has a B.Tech (Hons.), a PGCE and has been at East Court since 1992.

Susan Flory

Sue teaches PE, Art and Drama, but also assesses and develops programmes for our dyspraxic children. She has a Certificate in Education, a Diploma in Adaptive Physical Education and has been at East Court since 1989.

Gillian Gilmour

Gill is a specialist English teacher taking small groups for written language. She has a BA in Child Psychology and Comparative Religion, a Diploma from the Dyslexia Institute (AMBDA) and has been at East Court since 1989.

Marian McCormick

Marian is a speech therapist and takes children on a withdrawal basis as well as liaising and advising the English staff. She has a Masters degree in Human Communication and has been at East Court since 1997. She is developing the alphabetic system mentioned in her chapter, into a phonological training programme.

Rosemary Scott

Rosemary is a co-founder of East Court (1982) and is a counsellor at the school as well as the school bursar. She has a doctorate in Psychology and is a BAC accredited counsellor. She is writing a book on counselling and dyslexia due in 2003.

Michael Thomson

Michael is a co-founder of East Court (1982) and is the school's principal as well as teaching English. He has a doctorate in Psychology and is a Chartered Psychologist. He has published widely on dyslexia, including the *Aston Index* (co-author 1978), *Developmental Dyslexia* (1984, 1990), *Dyslexia: A Teaching Handbook* (co-author, 1999) and *The Psychology of Dyslexia: A Handbook for Teachers* (2001).

John Weavers

John is a mathematics teacher and has, along with other maths staff, developed the maths curriculum for our dyslexics. He has a Certificate in Education and a Diploma in Special Needs, and has been at East Court since 1993. John regularly lectures on INSET courses and conferences nationally.

Acknowledgements

Yonnette Ward for transcribing the initial chapters, floppy discs, different typefaces, scribblings on bits of paper and other random components, into a unified text. A lot of this was done during her holiday period – above and beyond the call of duty, thank you.

Sue Lade for taking time out of her busy office schedule to sort, organise and edit the final drafts.

Thank you also to the children at East Court who have helped us to learn how to help them over the years.

Preface

This book has arisen out of a workshop given at the British Dyslexia Association International Conference in York 2001. A number of East Court school staff contributed to this workshop and, as a result of the positive feedback received, we ran a weekend course at the school. The book is essentially a more formal, written version of these events. We have always tried to be a centre of excellence and to disseminate our teaching methods. As a specialist school for dyslexic children, we have the expertise and focus to develop approaches that we feel will help dyslexic children and we can monitor the results to see what is most effective.

The book is a practical one, although some theoretical background is given from time to time. We are sharing what we find has worked with our children; where possible we have given details to enable the reader to develop a programme but, given the space available, sometimes this is by example or overview. The book is primarily aimed at teachers and learning support staff who help dyslexic children. However, it will also be helpful for professionals such as speech therapists, psychologists or occupational therapists as well as parents of dyslexic children (some of whom overlap with the above).

We deliberately have not just focused on written language teaching, but have included other aspects to reinforce the nature of a whole-school approach.

The title *Dyslexia Included* refers to the recent emphasis on inclusion of special educational needs in the ordinary classroom. There will always be a need for specialist school provision, but most teachers will need to deal with dyslexia within the classroom or in a unit/withdrawal situation. 'Included' also refers to the inclusion of the difficulties, other than written language, that beset many dyslexics. How can we include them in our mathematics, ICT, humanities and games curricula? What specific problems do they bring to their personal development in specific subjects and around the school, and how can we help them? These are some of the areas we hope to tackle in this book. The reader should note as there is a ratio of four boys to one girl with dyslexic difficulties, the word 'he' has been used throughout when referring to pupils.

The first two chapters are on written language teaching; then we cover mathematics, ICT, general curriculum teaching, motor development/dyspraxia and counselling. I have written brief comments at the beginning of each chapter.

Finally, I would like to thank the staff at East Court who have contributed to this book. Putting yourself in print is hard work, particularly if you are not used to it, and it can be nerve-wracking to put your own ideas on the line.

Michael Thomson
September 2002

1 Continents and valves: an evidence-based approach to dyslexia

Marian McCormick

Marian sees her role as 'unplugging' the phonology of our children. This chapter starts off with an overview of some important theoretical approaches relating speech to phonological (sound) coding and written language. She then describes an approach to observation, assessment and remediation for those severe 'non-starting' dyslexics, who need help in basic sound-symbol associations. The focus is on the beginning stages and having the most theoretical material, makes this a natural first chapter. The title 'Continents and valves' refers to an East Court child's version of 'consonants and vowels'.

> Spelling in alphabetic scripts essentially means representing speech sounds. Thus spelling is visible phonology.
>
> (Frith 1980)

Have you ever looked at a child's draft written work and felt your stomach lurch as you see in front of you evidence of seemingly undigested spelling rules and word lists? Have you felt despair mount as you examine spellings taught on numerous occasions or corrected repeatedly over months? Experienced a rising panic as you become gradually aware that the spelling errors that you had hoped would lessen as the child developed are not only still present, but show little sign of improvement despite your concerted efforts?

Dyslexic children can demonstrate a wide range of spelling patterns within the space of one piece of work. These can range from complex words correctly spelt to spellings that are interpretable but creative; to indistinguishable words or 'small' words which have been taught many times, but can still be difficult to decipher in the context of an essay.

Looking at children's spellings can shed light on:

- what they understand about how the sounds of their language work;
- which sounds they consider to be similar to one another, and which sounds they consider to be different;
- how they build sounds into larger units such as syllables and words;
- how many sounds they can hear in a word;
- which sorts of sounds or combinations of sounds they will not be able to spell because they do not recognise them as individual units.

This chapter is aimed at teachers who have children whose difficulties with early literacy development are persistent or pronounced; who do not respond to the techniques and materials that have been proven to be effective with large numbers of other children; and who appear to be losing both ground and confidence. It does not pretend to offer a fail-safe solution, but shares a practical approach that has been tried and tested in the classroom with some of our most severe dyslexics.

Brief theoretical background

> One of the most important underlying explanations (of dyslexia) . . . is that there is a linguistic problem, in particular a phonological weakness, that impairs

> the process of learning to read and spell . . . an impairment to a phonological processing system that is not dedicated to reading or spelling tasks per se, but is used in all forms of phonological tasks . . . Some of the most characteristic indicators of phonological problems are the following:
>
> - problems in segmenting words into phonemes
> - problems in keeping linguistic material (strings of sounds or letters) in short-term memory
> - problems in repeating back long non-words
> - problems in reading and writing even short non-words.
>
> (Lundberg and Hoien 2001)

1. Literacy and speech

Although the typical dyslexic can 'talk', there exists a strong relationship between children's acquisition of literacy and their phonological or sound processing skills. Children with literacy problems often have difficulties with speech and language development. In some children these difficulties are easy to spot, as their words can be difficult to understand, especially in conversation. In others, the signs are less distinct, becoming obvious only when the child tries to say a long or unfamiliar word. For a few, the underlying difficulties with language processing only become evident when they need to try to find a particular word to express an idea, recall the name of a person or object, or become confused about the meanings of words that sound very similar.

Children with speech and language difficulties often experience problems with learning to read and spell; the difficulties in their speech and language are frequently reflected or reproduced in their reading and spelling attempts; or become evident as they try to understand the written word.

Research has consistently found a high degree of correlation between these two sets of skills.

> The high rate of co-occurrence for speech, language and literacy problems arises from the fact that each have their roots in the same speech processing system; established to deal with the demands of the spoken language system, it is later exploited to support the acquisition of literacy skills.
>
> (Stackhouse and Wells 1997)

2. Speech and phonological processing

The speech processing system forms part of the language centres of the brain. It is a general term, which refers to all the skills included in understanding and producing speech. It is primarily involved in the development of spoken language, and is only later used to support the acquisition of literacy skills.

Phonological processing skills are part of the larger speech processing system. They are involved in the identification, recognition, analysis and production of speech sounds – picking up small but significant differences between words; categorising, sorting and sequencing them for understanding, storage and use; setting up phonological representations in the mind. The phonological system is built around the development of sounds (phonemes) and the relationships between them.

There are two basic relationships: sequential and contrastive.

Sequential relationships are those that involve the left–right organisation of sounds. Sequences of letters have different meanings when organised in different sequential relationship to one another: for example apt, tap, pat; stop, post, tops; shelf, flesh.

Contrastive relationships are those in which the child substitutes sounds which he views as having similar features:

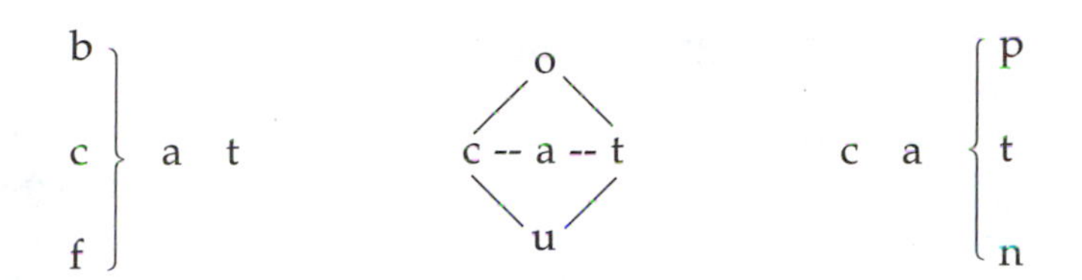

or f-in instead of th-in, g-oat instead of c-oat.

These relationships are important for both speech and spelling as the majority of spelling errors will reflect problems in one or other of these basic concepts, and it is therefore a useful means by which to categorise difficulties.

3. Phonological processing skills and early literacy development

The acquisition of literacy skills makes different demands on the child's processing skills at different points of the developmental progression. At each critical stage the child must bring specialised resources to the learning situation if the development of literacy is to proceed. If the child does not, for whatever reason, have access to these resources, they will be at risk of compromising their progress to the next developmental stage, or being able to learn the skills inherent in that developmental stage.

Phonological processing skills are seen as cognitive prerequisites – specialised resources or essential skills – for the successful development of skilled reading and spelling. They act as a bridge between speech sounds and letters.

Phonological processing skills are characteristically weak in dyslexic children as they have difficulty in abstracting letter-sound correspondences from the printed word, and therefore fail to develop phonological (phonic) reading and spelling strategies.

4. Stages of development

Many children begin to read by recognising whole words, and then they gradually become aware of the relationship between letters and the speech sounds they represent. This growing understanding of these correspondences is called the alphabetic principle. Most theoretical accounts of literacy acquisition have proposed a succession of developmental stages, which are characterised by distinctive patterns of strategy use (Marsh *et al.*, 1980; Ehri, 1991).

Frith (1985) proposes a three-stage sequence of development. The first stage is called the **logographic stage**, which is characterised by the use of visual recognition of whole words. Children begin to associate whole words with their meaning by remembering prominent visual features, such as the position of letters and shape of the word, and establishing other arbitrary links between a word and its meaning. It is essentially non-analytic, and relies on visual memory. Non-phonetic spelling attempts indicate that the child has grasped the idea that a string of letters can represent a word; however there is no attempt to represent the sound of the word by use of letters.

Stackhouse and Wells (1997) describe an intermediate stage where the child begins to demonstrate an ability to link, or segment, the initial sound of a word with its letter, e.g. 'p' for pig.

The second stage is called the **alphabetic stage**, which is concerned with the development of the relationship between sounds and letters. This stage is dependent upon auditory processing. Chiat (1979) argued that the most important task facing children, both in learning the phonology of their language and in literacy development, is first to isolate meaningful units and then to work out how those units differ from one another – sequential and contrastive relationships. This involves the child's ability to identify, segment, analyse, and break the word into its component structures; the large (syllable) and small (phoneme) segments of the word – speech sounds. Words are not instantly recognised in reading but the child can, by sounding out sequential letters, arrive at the pronunciation of regular words. Spelling at this stage is also carried out in a linear fashion, with one letter for each sound.

The final stage is called the **orthographic stage** and it is marked by another strategy change, this time involving 'chunks' of language information – morphemes – such as *- tion*, *- ed*, *- ing*. This stage also uses primarily visual processing skills as in the logographic stage, but the two stages are differentiated by the analytic nature of orthographic analysis.

Although these three different stages are described as emerging in a strict developmental order, the strategies used at one stage are not suppressed when the child adopts new strategies that mark progression to a later developmental stage. These remain as resources in the repertoire of skilled readers and spellers. The use of earlier strategies declines as later ones assume prominence.

According to Frith (1985), a primary characteristic of a dyslexic child is their difficulty, or failure, in making the transition between the whole word visual processing of the logographic stage to the phonological processing required for negotiation of the alphabetic stage. This has been termed the 'alphabetic barrier'.

> We need to teach children with specific learning difficulties exactly those skills which they find most difficult. This implies having to overcome the 'alphabetic barrier' by teaching them the relationship between sound and symbol in order that the child may recognise new words, pick up grapheme-phoneme conversion links, develop segmentation and syllabic skills and all the fundamental substrate of the structured programs which are commonly used.
>
> (Thomson and Watkins 1998)

Examples of errors from different spelling stages are given in Table 1.1.

5. Mapping

The formation of mapping relationships is crucial to this stage of development. Mappings reflect a child's organisation and understanding of how the sounds of language 'fit' onto letters.

> In the alphabetic stage, connections are gradually set up between all letters in a word, and the phonemic constituents of the word's pronunciation. These connections not only link individual letters or digraphs with phonemes, but allow the pronunciation of sequences of letters to be accessed.
>
> (Ehri 1992)

At the earliest stages of literacy acquisition these mappings and relationships are fundamental to the emerging written language system. Dyslexic children frequently have difficulty in making these connections, and working out the relationship between letters and sounds.

> Dyslexic children are seen as having deficits at the level of phonological representations which compromise their ability to set up mappings between orthography and phonology.
>
> (Snowling 2000)

Some children have a very limited capacity for holding a string of sounds in their short-term memory, or listening to a word and being able to tell how many sounds there are in the word, or even which sounds they can hear. This makes spelling very difficult.

> Many dyslexic children are insensitive to such phonological connections and treat each word as if it is unique; they therefore have no schema for organizing and generalizing.
>
> (Krupska and Klein 1998)

6. Phonological awareness and phonological processing skills

Before children begin to learn how to read and spell, they have usually already learnt

Table 1.1 Examples of errors from various spelling stages (Data taken from work at East Court and a mainstream primary school)

Target word (Standard adult spelling)	*Orthographic*	*Phonemic*	*Semi-phonemic*	*Metaphonemic*	*Non-phonemic*
fish	phish	fis	fit/firch	fllts	s
puppy	pupy	pupe	pup	puet	bcpns
tulip	tullip	cholip	choop	tup	stuncds
polish	pollish	pullish	posh	pch	nutbe
refreshment	reafreshment	rfeshmet	refrsmt	ffmet	lletp
instructed	instruckted	instudid	insrud	isd	tents
Target words taken and analysis derived from Snowling and Stackhouse (1996).	Evident within this set of spellings is the emergence of orthographic spelling rules. Patterns transcend the one sound–one letter relationship of the alphabetic stage and show more complex relations and use of morphemes.	The phonemic stage is shown by the representation of a one-to-one correspondence between sounds and letters. A key feature of this stage is the representation of stressed vowel segments.	These spellings show a growing awareness of the salient sounds within words – some vowel sounds are indicated; initial and final sounds are marked, with the occasional medial consonant.	These spellings demonstrate the emergence of metaphonological awareness (Stackhouse and Wells 1987). The early stages of sound–letter correspondences can be seen in the correct transcription of the initial sound of the word.	These letter strings bear no discernible relationship to the target word, and are categorised as non-phonemic responses.

how to make and use the speech sounds of their language, by means of their phonological processing skills. They have implicit knowledge about the nature of the phonological system of their language. When faced with the challenge of learning to read and spell, they need to tap into that knowledge and be able to reflect on it. This ability to think about, and use, what they know is called **phonological awareness** – the ability to attend to the components of the word, and concentrate on its sound structure rather than its visual form or meaning.

> Implicit language knowledge involves the abstraction and use of linguistic rules, whereas explicit knowledge involves the ability to examine those rules at a conscious level.
>
> (Cooper 1985)

Clinical experience suggests that there are three main levels of phonological coding skills.

Swimmers: Those who will learn to read and spell almost in spite of the strategies and material presented to them. They appear to have a natural ability to infer and assimilate written language. Their progress is usually rapid and straightforward.

Flounderers: Those who may be considered to have a developmental delay. 'They are not ready to read at the expected time within the present educational system, but their phonological difficulties are mild. So it is possible that with maturity they will gradually develop along normal lines . . . if phonic teaching has been stressed' (Snowling 1987). This is a group who can learn to read and spell if provided with a structured, systematic and cumulative system.

Drowners: Those who have significant difficulties in processing written language information. These children require specialised help and resources in order to facilitate their literacy development. These difficulties, which can be severe, arise from specific deficits in phonological processing skills, and maturation alone will not lead to the resolution of these problems.

Our programme takes a developmental approach, and can be used with both 'flounderers', and 'drowners'. It aims to provide the child with the foundational phonological skills needed for the successful negotiation of the alphabetic stage.

Assessment

The first job is to begin to unravel the strands of what is difficult and why. In order to do this you need to collect some evidence.

Collecting the evidence

The aim of this assessment is to identify those children for whom weak phonological processing skills are contributing significantly to their literacy problems. This is not dependent on the age of the child, but relates more to:

- the developmental stage acquired;
- the level of skill development within that stage;
- the predominant processing strategies exhibited.

As such it should identify those children who have good visual skills, but who appear to have immature or poorly developed phonological skills.

The assessment described below is an adjunct to the more usual ability, attainment and diagnostic assessment (e.g. Thomson 2001). It is classroom-based and ongoing.

A format is given for collecting a core set of data, but any spelling attempts gathered at home or at school can be added to that core to provide a more complete picture of the child's performance and of their progress. This gives flexibility, helps to ensure a representative sample, and provides a means for parents to be actively involved in the process.

Defining the problem

The primary aims of the assessment are to:

- identify the level at which the child does *not* fail;
- identify recurring patterns in the child's spelling attempts;
- indicate which of these patterns requires intervention in order to achieve more effective written communication;
- determine the predominant processing strategies used by the child, and therefore the appropriate level of intervention.

Most standardised assessments can provide a wealth of information and an overall picture of levels of attainment in comparison with a peer group, but are not usually designed to be sensitive to qualitative changes such as developmental progression or strategy use – changes in the nature of the child's responses. Many children with moderate to severe phonological difficulties are not able to score even at the lowest levels on such tests. Even with extensive test results it is sometimes hard to translate them into a tangible plan of action or treatment for the child – the information is interesting but not immediately or obviously applicable to the teaching situation.

This approach is based on the premise by Thomson and Watkins (1998) that 'assessment should be both functional and directive'. Figure 1.1 illustrates the points discussed below.

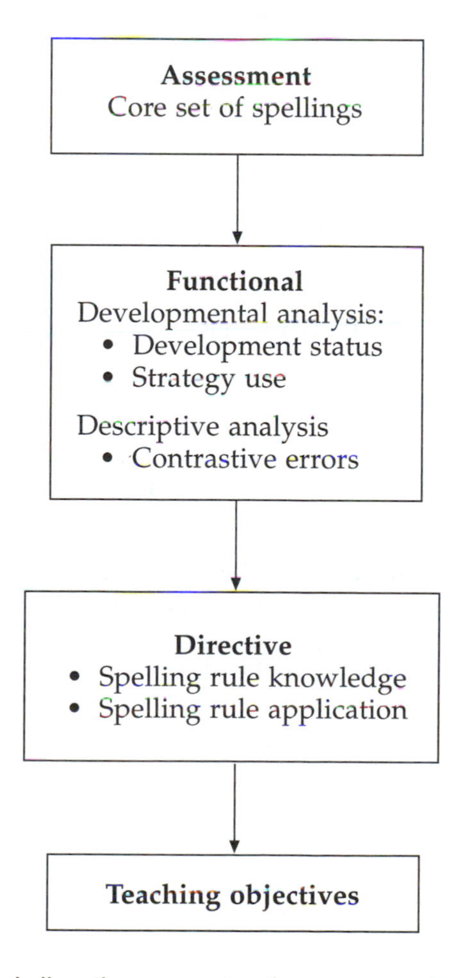

Figure 1.1 Functional and directive aspects of assessment

Functional assessment

This helps focus on what is hampering learning. It looks at:

How does the child learn? What levels of processing and cognitive skills does he bring to the task?
What does he do with the skills he has? How does he apply them to the task of learning to read and spell? What strategies has he developed?

Directive assessment

This aims to show what needs to be learnt and in some cases what needs to be unlearnt. It looks at how the child's representation of the word differs from the word he intended to write and the relationship between the two. There will be a relationship – sometimes it may be weak or obscure, but the majority of children will be systematic/predictable as to the nature of their error patterns, as those patterns reflect their internal organisation of phonemic information. Assessment also needs to be **dynamic**, in that each interaction with a child can either provide more clues as to the nature and extent of their difficulties, or confirm the progress they are making. Non-standard spelling attempts are clues as to how the child is processing information, and the nature of the impediment to progress.

Collecting a core set of data

A minimum sample should consist of:

- spelling errors taken from a piece of spontaneous writing;
- a set of words varying in syllable length;
- a set of phonically regular words and non-words, such as 'Alphabetics screening test'.

Although this may seem a large time commitment, such simple spelling tests are quick and easy to administer and can be done as a whole class, small group or on an individual basis.

Making sense of it all

The primary role for phonic skills is to enable the child to read and spell unfamiliar words. This relies on the ability to:

- segment words into their component parts;
- analyse the relationships between the sounds, working out how they differ from one another – sequential and constrastive features – which require sequencing and categorisation skills.

Once a core set of spellings has been gathered, the next step is to analyse them according to the above criteria and to gather information about how successfully the child is able to carry out these operations. This again requires an investment of time in the short term, but can lead to precise and easy-to-monitor teaching objectives.

Take the words that have been spelled incorrectly and categorise them according to how far they are away from the standard spelling: one easy means of doing this is to look at the word out of context and see how hard it is to decipher without clues as to its meaning. The more help you need, the less **phonemic referencing** there is. Spellings can be categorised as:

1. Standard
2. Orthographic
3. Phonemic
4. Semi-phonemic

5. Meta-phonemic
6. Non-phonemic.

See Table 1.1 for an example of a completed record sheet.

Each of these categories reflects a particular level of dealing with phonemic information, and thus can be very useful in determining the developmental status of the child's spelling patterns. The less phonemic referencing evident in a child's spelling patterns, the more severe their phonological processing problems tend to be.

There are two forms of analysis that are particularly useful when looking for clues within the child's spelling patterns.

Developmental analysis

1. Identifies the differences between the adult spellings and the child's response. How close to the adult target does the spelling come?
2. Provides an indication of the developmental status of the child's spelling patterns, and strategy use. An example from an actual child (TP) is given in Figure 1.2.

Developmental analysis				
Example: TP (see also case study later)				
Target	Orthographic	Phonemic	Semi-phonemic	Non-phonemic
private			prut	
plane*		blan		
flight		flit		
started			sate	
rain		ran		
screen		scren		
lightning			litnig	

This analysis of TP's spelling patterns shows some important features:

- He is able to use phonemic strategies when spelling one-syllable words.
- His phonemic strategies have not yet evolved sufficiently to mark long as opposed to short vowel sounds.
- When confronted with less familiar, or longer two-syllable words his strategies fall back to semi-phonemic patterns.
- *plane – blan. This type of error pattern has been highlighted as it occurs frequently within TP's core set of data. An analysis is included in the descriptive assessment.

Figure 1.2 Developmental analysis

Descriptive analysis

As you enter the spellings, look for relationships among the data you have collected. Often, as you look, a pattern begins to emerge, and will provide clues as to the underlying nature of the spelling errors. This type of analysis:

1. Provides a description of the patterns in the child's attempts in terms of sequential/structural and contrastive error patterns.
2. Provides a framework for the identification of disordered patterns. How easy is it for the reader to read or interpret the words?
3. Facilitates the development of treatment aims. Where the patterns are assessed to be problematic, the analysis should indicate which patterns need to be modified in order for the child to achieve more functional patterns.
4. Identifies and evaluates changes in the child's spelling patterns when a second analysis is performed after a period of treatment. (Adapted from Grunwell 1985.)

Figures 1.3 and 1.4 illustrate the functional and directive approaches with consequent analysis.

Descriptive assessment 1					
Example: TP					
Structural/Sequential			Contrastive		
Target	Response		Target	Response	
monster	mons		plane	blan	p–b
			cave	gave	c–g
			pilot	bilat	p–b
			great	cret	g–c
			breakfast	precfact	b–p
			pointed	bot	p–b
			TP has consistent difficulty in hearing the difference between similar sounds, voiced and voiceless consonants, when they occur at the beginning of words. This is not a simple matter of confusing graphemes b/d, p/b, or letter reversals, but a recurrent error pattern.		
TP shows evidence of wide-based phonemic processing problems with multiple errors in both structural and contrastive levels of analysis.					

Figure 1.3 Descriptive assessment 1

Descriptive assessment 2						
Example: CK						
Structural				Contrastive		
trust	tust	ccvcc	cvcc	slipped	slep	
tramp	tamp	ccvcc	cvcc	lift	left	
lunch	luch	cvcc	cvc	fist	fet*	
lump	lup	cvccc	cvcc			
bench	bech	cvcc	cvc			
bump	bup	cvcc	cvc			
There is evidence of two main types of error in this set of data: 1. Reduction of word initial blends. 2. Reduction of word final blends involving nasal consonants.				1. Vowel transcription errors; 'i'–'e' 2. *Although this error would be classified as semi-phonemic, it could be addressed by targeting the two processes of final blends and vowel errors.		
Contrastive errors are of a relatively low rate of occurrence in CK's data. The most significant error base is in his difficulty in segmenting consonant blends.						

Figure 1.4 Descriptive assessment 2

The next pages provide worked examples from two children, each of whom has a differing level of ability.

The first child, AK, came to the school at age 9.6. His difficulties were severe. His written output was low, word boundaries were not recognised nor marked, and his spontaneous writing was unintelligible. Basic letter-sound bonds were not consistent, and he had no reliable transcription of short vowels.

AK was able to accurately and consistently identify and use only a small group of letter-sound bonds. He was not able to blend two sounds together to make a simple syllable. If presented with a word such as 'up', he would sound out the individual letters, even after demonstration, and be unable to combine the segments into a word that he could recognise. Another feature of his performance at this time was the instability of his representations – in attempting to blend two sounds, which he had shown himself able to recognise individually, he would, during the attempt, alter one or more characteristics of that sound. This phonemic instability was a significant factor in his lack of progress in developing alphabetic skills.

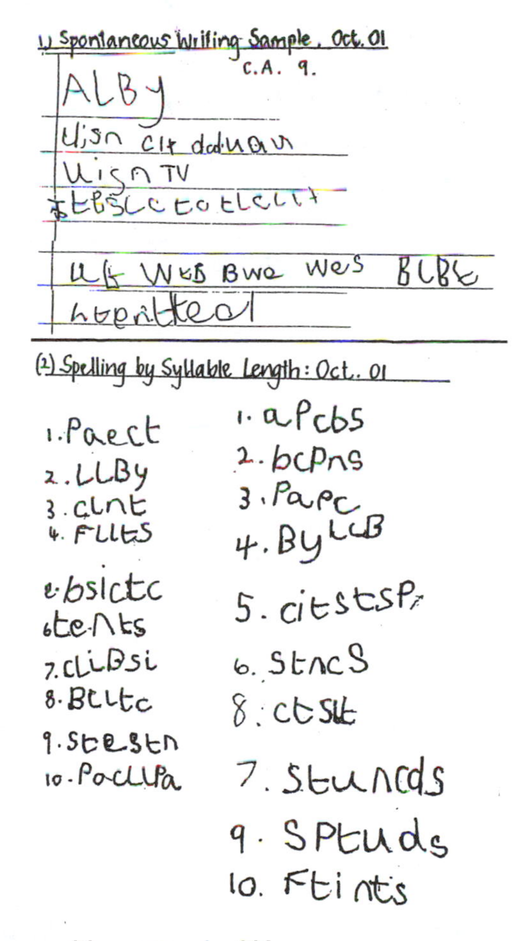

Figure 1.5 Spontaneous writing sample AK

The second child, TP, was 11 years old when he was referred. He had initially made good progress but this had not been sustained. His profile was somewhat different, in that on initial observation he seemed to be functioning at quite a high level, his written output was high, with complex language structures and evidence of an advanced vocabulary for his age. However, assessment showed that his phonological processing skills were very weak, with a high proportion of his spellings indecipherable. The strategy employed by the teacher was to encourage him to write only one or two sentences before reading it aloud to a member of staff so that they could transcribe above it the identity of the words. In this way the content of the story was able to be preserved, and his level of vocabulary use appreciated. Figure 1.6 shows samples of writing and spelling.

TP was able to cope consistently with only three pieces of sound information, and had been supplementing his written vocabulary by use of his excellent visual memory skills.

This could only be a short-term solution for him, as his vocabulary was so extensive that the strain on his memory skills led to a high incidence of visual and sequencing errors. His phonological strategies for attacking unfamiliar words were very limited.

TP showed some ability to read and spell words beginning with consonant blends, but this was not consistent and was related in part to his familiarity with the word, rather than its structure. Thus he was assessed as being able to achieve a 100 per cent success rate at the consonant-vowel-consonant (CVC) level. Errors began to appear at the CCVC level.

The majority of the words analysed fell into the semi-phonemic category, suggesting that TP had a difficulty with large segment or syllable segmentation.

(1) Spontaneous Writing Sample: June 02 Name: T.P. C.A:

the mons swam to wocks me ~~the bot~~ I ran to the 9
corpit and fond my brysot and buving kat I brow the in fla 22
jacut in to the wat I toot my und water carm I burd in 36
just bfar the mons jos in golft the tramsm I clipt my jacet 49
and swam as fast ~~as~~ I can wont my fet were on the ~~grond~~ pele 63
I cod not see enthing and len I sor all of the ness monster 77
I cort It all on carm I sorr my bot seind in fron of me
and ~~then~~ then I lond to see the gaping mot of the lacnet
sucked 104

(2) Spelling by Syllable Length: May 02

1	Pet	appoll	membsip	msterest
2	lip	pupy	sigrel	msheenre
3	cap	pacet	callock	polleson
4	fish	trumpet	seplenb	congrathlat
5	sack	uton	advench	jogfre
6	tent	trafik	Undstand	magnifsont
7	trap	calle	conlent	cadelor
8	bump	chodlip	rfeshmont	discovey
9	nest	polish	instruct	radat
10	bank	fing	unprell	olmat

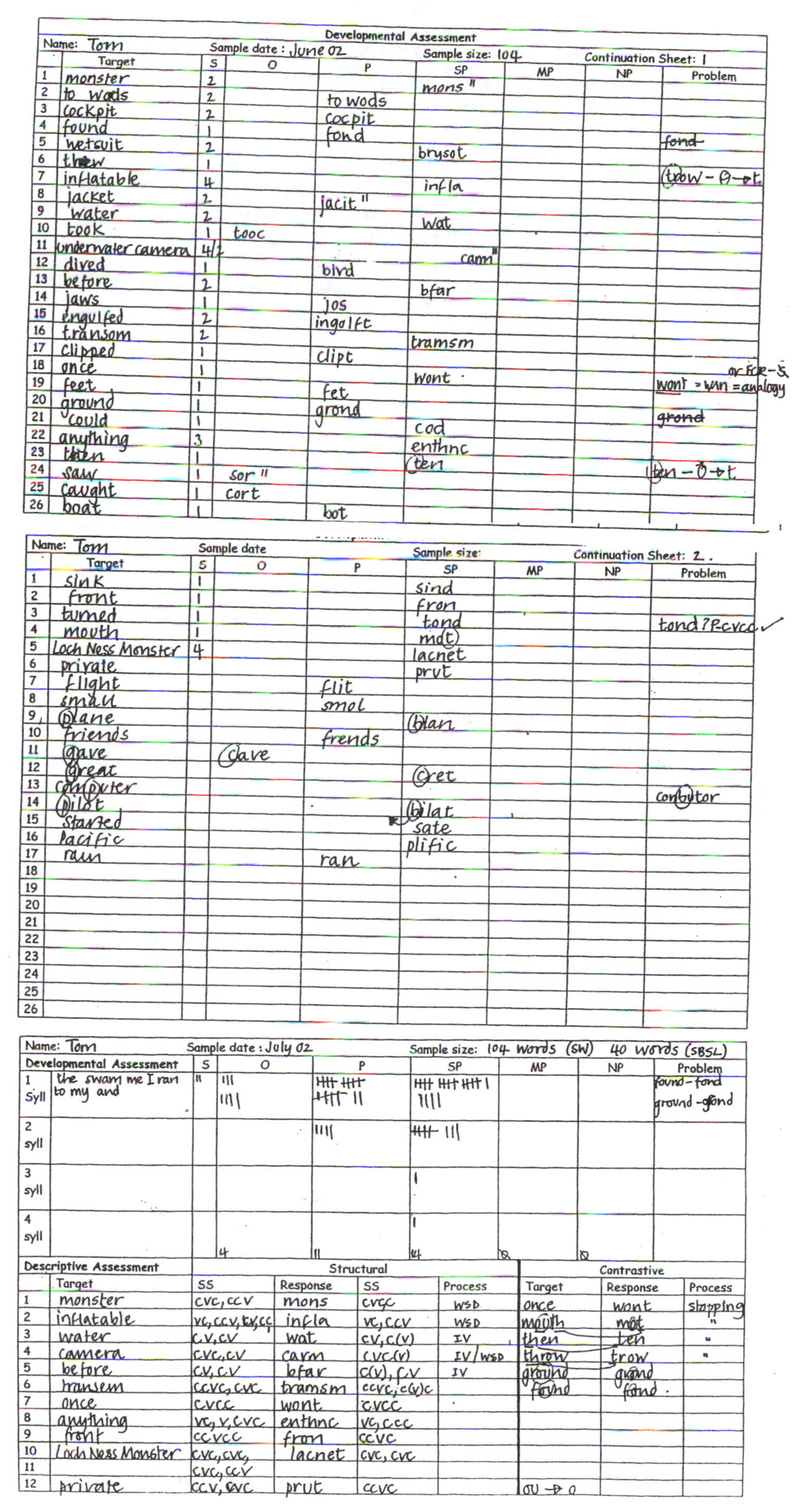

Developmental Assessment

Name: Tom Sample date: June 02 Sample size: 104 Continuation Sheet: 1

	Target	S	O	P	SP	MP	NP	Problem
1	monster	2			mons "			
2	to wards	2		to wods				
3	cockpit	2		cocpit				
4	found	1		fond				fond
5	wetsuit	2			brysot			
6	threw	1						(t)row – θ→t
7	inflatable	4			infla			
8	jacket	2		jacit "				
9	water	2			wat			
10	took	1	tooc					
11	underwater camera	4/2			camm"			
12	dived	1		bird				
13	before	2			bfar			
14	jaws	1		jos				
15	engulfed	2		ingolft				
16	transom	2			tramsm			
17	clipped	1		clipt				
18	once	1			wont			wont = wan = analogy or fcr-5
19	feet	1		fet				
20	ground	1		grond				grond
21	could	1			cod			
22	anything	3			enthnc			
23	then	1			(t)en			(t)en – θ→t
24	saw	1	sor "					
25	caught	1	cort					
26	boat	1		bot				

Name: Tom Sample date Sample size: Continuation Sheet: 2.

	Target	S	O	P	SP	MP	NP	Problem
1	sink	1			sind			
2	front	1			fron			
3	turned	1			tond			tond?P-cvcc ✓
4	mouth	1			mo(t)			
5	Loch Ness Monster	4			lacnet			
6	private				prvt			
7	flight			flit				
8	small			smol				
9	(p)lane				(b)lan			
10	friends			frends				
11	(g)ave		(c)lave					
12	(g)reat				(c)ret			
13	computer							con(b)tor
14	(p)ilot				(b)ilat			
15	started				sate			
16	Pacific				plific			
17	rain			ran				
18								
19								
20								
21								
22								
23								
24								
25								
26								

Name: Tom Sample date: July 02 Sample size: 104 words (SW) 40 words (SBSL)

Developmental Assessment		S	O	P	SP	MP	NP	Problem
1 Syll	the swam me I ran to my and	II	III IIII	HHT HHT HHT II	HHT HHT HHT I IIII			found – fond; ground – grond
2 syll				IIII	HHT III			
3 syll					I			
4 syll			4	11	14	0	0	

Descriptive Assessment

	Target	SS	Response	SS	Process	Target	Response	Process
		Structural				Contrastive		
1	monster	cvc, ccv	mons	cvcc	WSD	once	wont	stopping
2	inflatable	vc, ccv, cv, cc	infla	vc, ccv	WSD	mouth	mot	"
3	water	cv, cv	wat	cv, c(v)	IV	then	ten	"
4	camera	cvc, cv	carm	cvc(v)	IV/WSD	throw	trow	"
5	before	cv, cv	bfar	c(v), cv	IV	ground	grond	
6	transom	ccvc, cvc	tramsm	ccvc, c(v)c		found	fond	
7	once	cvcc	wont	cvcc				
8	anything	vc, v, cvc	enthnc	vc, ccc				
9	front	ccvcc	fron	ccvc				
10	Loch Ness Monster	cvc, cvc,	lacnet	cvc, cvc				
11		cvc, ccv						
12	private	ccv, cvc	prvt	ccvc		ou → o		

Figure 1.6 Various writing sample TP

Children may exhibit more than one level of strategy. For example, TP's predominant developmental strategy is semi-phonemic, but he also demonstrates phonemic and orthographic error patterns in the course of his work, which reflect learnt spelling patterns and emergent skills. This is entirely normal, as dyslexia is a developmental disorder, and as such has an inherently dynamic nature. The baseline, however, becomes evident when we consider the primary function of phonological skills in the role of the skilled reader and speller – that of processing unfamiliar words. When a child is faced with an unfamiliar word, or when the processing demands of a task exceed his processing capacity, he will resort to tapping into his phonological resources – simplification processes – in order to complete the task. It is at this point that the integrity of the system, the baseline level of skill, is exposed. A third example of descriptive assessment, that of EG, is given in Figure 1.7, where the main difficulty is very specific, namely consonant digraphs.

Descriptive assessment 3							
Example: EG							
Structural				Contrastive			
				chickens	thikings	ch	th
				tulip	thulep	ch	th
				finger	thing	f	th
				refreshment	rethement	fr sh	th O
				brothers	bruves	th	v
				chappatis	ypatey	ch	y
				mushrooms	musrums	sh	s
1. No significant or consistent structural difficulties.				1. EG's main area of difficulty lies in poorly defined representations of consonant digraphs.			
EG shows well-developed phonemic-level skills. He represents each segment with a vowel and maintains syllable structure. Contrastive difficulties involve a relatively small group of phonemic contrasts.							

Figure 1.7 Descriptive Assessment 3

'Where do I start?'

> Before students can practice they must first learn how to do it. Just because they are exposed to material doesn't necessarily mean they learn from it.
>
> (Vail 1992)

> Since the primary factor dictating progress is phonological skill then early intervention to promote this vital resource is an obvious necessity.
>
> (Snowling 1987)

The evidence-based approach:

- Helps to identify those areas that provide the biggest barriers to the child's progress. These may not always be the same as the curriculum goals, nor the next developmental step.
- Uses each interaction with the child as an opportunity to provide more clues about the nature and extent of their difficulties; or to confirm the progress they are making.

- Teaches to errors. Non-standard spellings are seen as clues as to how the child is dealing with the information presented. Teaching is directly influenced by the child's response to the strategies and tasks.
- Encourages children to take responsibility for aspects of their own learning. To understand:
  - what their target is
  - what their strengths are
  - how they learn most effectively
  - how to reflect on their progress.

There is often little guidance as to how to approach spelling errors – whether to correct or not; what to correct – all or nothing? Perhaps something in between? If it is the something in between option, how do you know which ones to choose out of the array of errors you find in front of you? Are some more serious than others? Should it be those that were in last week's spelling test, that looked all right then, but obviously are not now? What about the ones that are barely decipherable?

In order to know if something is disordered, one has to know something of what normal development, or normal developmental patterns, look like. This provides a reference point for knowing if it is time to panic or to wait for him to grow out of it. It also provides a rough index of which patterns are the most worrying, and therefore form the most pressing teaching objectives.

Returning to our three indices of the nature and severity of problems with the alphabetic stage of development:

- phonemic segmentation span
- syllable length and complexity
- developmental strategy

there are some broad guidelines that can be followed:

- The further away from the adult standard a spelling falls on the categorisation, the more in need of attention it is.
- The aim should be to introduce and practise the skills necessary to the child and to explore and understand the reason why a particular spelling is difficult to understand.
- Aim to discover what the pattern underlying that type of error is, and therefore why he has a tendency to make similar errors.
- Aim to learn how to change what he is doing to ensure that he is more successful in getting over exactly what he wants to express/spell so that his primary aim – communication – can be achieved.

This approach is based on phonological principles. It assumes that consistent and sustained progress is more likely to occur when the techniques used address the needs of the child's processing system – the 'cause' – rather than focusing on the spelling errors – the symptoms. A child can be presented with a spelling list, rehearse it and reproduce it successfully in a spelling test, yet will return to his original version in a piece of written work the following day because the exercise had not altered the way the spelling was categorised or registered on his 'hardware' – the internal dictionary where word information is stored for retrieval. In order to try to address this problem – to try to alter how the child deals with sound information – a system has been developed at the school, which takes the child through three different levels of phonological learning:

- concept development
- exploratory learning
- extended practice and integration of new and acquired knowledge and skills.

Differentiation of these three stages has been found to be very effective with children with moderate to severe levels of difficulty.

The programme aims to teach the child both the basis of what is predictable and consistent within the written language system – in terms of letter/sound correspondences – and processes for applying that knowledge. The structure of the skill development programme means that the child is consistently able to succeed.

ICE (Introduction, Consolidation and Extension) Skill Development Programme

The programme developed at school has been devised to provide appropriate material across all levels of syllable complexity as a resource to this end. Each level represents a conceptual step, either a change in syllabic complexity or the introduction of new phoneme/grapheme relationships. There is a developmental progression both between the levels of the programme as well as within each level.

1. Introduction

The aim of this stage is to discuss with the child what you are going to ask them to learn; why it is important for them to learn it; and how it relates to what they already know.

This stage provides the child with:

- a context for learning;
- help to develop a vocabulary of terms with which to label the concepts they will be using;
- practice in recognising and identifying visual and auditory features which differentiate words from one another.

2. Consolidation

The main emphasis at this level is the notion of problem solving. The child is encouraged to actively explore small but significant differences between words in a structured teaching environment that will allow them to discover the basic principles for themselves. This can be carried out in either individual or small group sessions.

- Instruction is explicit.
- Only small amounts of new information are introduced at a time.
- Levels of difficulty for tasks are increased in small increments.
- Learning tasks are given immediate application.
- Prompt and specific feedback is given.
- Errors are treated as 'clues' – teaching points, which illustrate that the child has not yet grasped the skill or principle. Further examples at the same level or of the same genre are presented so that the child has the opportunity to work out how to master the point.

The three main skills to be mastered are:

- segmentation: initially onset-rime, progressing to the phoneme level;
- sequencing;
- categorisation: identifying patterns; rhyming tasks; alliteration games; phoneme manipulation tasks etc.

This stage is very hands-on and teaching sessions are mainly carried out using manipulatives: word cards; games formatted for use with word cards etc. Techniques such as guided experience, problem solving, discovery and forced alternatives can all be used.

- 'The same content is organized and presented in several different ways so students can select the activities that best suit their learning style.' (Reid 1998, p. 15).

- Worksheets are rarely used at this level, as the child needs explicit instruction and support in discovering the rules and relationships of this alphabetic stage of development. The child becomes actively involved in exploring words and focusing on small differences between words, increasing both their phonemic segmentation span and their lexical differentiation.

Non-words are introduced at this stage, as their use sheds light on the child's understanding of how individual letters map onto the speech sounds of written words and how robust that knowledge is.

- Dyslexic children have particular difficulty with such tasks, tending to rely extensively on visual processing strengths and linguistic guessing. These skills are important, and are employed by skilled readers, but those skilled readers have access also to the phonologically based analysis skills that the dyslexics do not.
- The use of non-words allows the teacher to see how the child is able to apply his phonic skills to novel words or letter strings, thus providing a useful way to assess both phonic reading and spelling skills.

3. Extension

This stage is only entered once the child can demonstrate confident mastery of the previous phase.

> While developing a skill there is a substantial amount of information-processing capacity focused on that skill, and associated factors, at that time. Typically, as fluency increases, less information-processing capacity needs to be allocated, and eventually the skill becomes automatic.
>
> (Samuels 1999 in Fawcett 2001)

The aim of this level is to develop confidence, accuracy and speed – that is the part of the learning process that allows consolidation of sub-skills. Children with dyslexia find developing automaticity difficult to achieve in tasks relating to phonological processing. Error identification and self-correction are also aims of this teaching level. Worksheets are used at this level, as are tasks that have timing as an element in them.

Many teachers report dyslexic children within the mainstream class as being very 'dependent' learners, requiring high levels of attention, feedback and support, and demanding of the teacher's time. There should be differentiation of these levels of working and the expectations associated with them – 'You are very good at working out CCVC words now, you can do the sheet I have given you. When you have finished it we can look at it together, and see what good work you've done.' Here the child has received explicit instruction at this particular level and has the skills to carry out the task independently. One of the aims of the extension stage is to convince him of this.

Increasing independence and self-reliance is an important aim in a busy classroom.

Making it work/Putting it into practice

Working with children who have experienced persistent difficulty or failure in learning to read and spell, means having to address certain issues before actually starting in with yet another lot of tasks for them to do – like having to unpick a piece of knitting when it has gone wrong, it needs to be taken back to the bit that was the right shape or size, and then moved forward from a place where you know it is as it should be.

Some of the unpicking that needs to go on involves issues of:

- expecting failure ('Why should I do that, I'm only going to get it wrong');
- guilt ('I haven't been able to do it, but everyone else can');
- defensiveness ('What makes you think you've got anything to offer that they haven't already tried?'), which can manifest as 'attitude';
- holding on to unconstructive learning patterns, on a security blanket basis ('I may not know much about reading and spelling, but at least I can do this!');
- lack of motivation ('Why should I?').

Many of the children who have prompted the writing of this chapter have at times expressed feelings of being overwhelmed at the size, complexity and seemingly endless amount of information they are required to take in. It seems that if we want to help them, these are some of the most pressing and important things to consider and address.

The primary aim is to help children to experience success at whatever level of reading and spelling development they are starting from. Some effective ways of dealing with 'unpicking' are as follows.

1. Provide a context for learning

- Be real about it. Talk about what you have found out about the nature of their literacy problems: identify the problem and then identify the steps needed to move forward.
- Present a clear structure. Put it all into context for them, give them the big picture and show them how it all fits together.
- Bring the task down to size. Provide a tangible set of steps/goals, which allows them to see where they are, where they are going and how it relates to where they have been. This helps them to feel safe and understand what is expected of them, however big they might be. It also helps to foster a sense of purpose.
- Describe each step. Have a point of completion, which leads to a reward. The importance of this is that they can experience tangible progress.

2. Make it relevant

These children need to know that what you are doing is relevant to their needs. Programmes that are externally imposed or curriculum-driven, without reference to the child's processing needs, have been shown to have a very limited effect. Strategies and learning objectives must be personalised and specific, based on analysis of their performance and the nature of their spelling errors. These act as clues as to how they are processing information. Start by showing them how much they already know, the skills they have already acquired, the rules they have learnt and can apply effectively. Then start exploring the gaps. Talk with them about the nature of their errors, what sort of mistakes they tend to make. Help them to understand that their errors may not be standard, but they are not random.

3. Involve them in the process

One of the prime aims is to build a secure framework from which they can go on to hang new learning and information. This is most likely to happen when the child appropriates the strategies. In order to do this, they must see them as useful and effective. They must therefore understand what they do that works, and why; and what they do that does not work, and why. Experiment with different strategies to find out which have the best results.

4. Let them know how they are doing

Provide immediate feedback that is specific and aimed at increasing the child's awareness of what works and what does not. If a particular type of error recurs, such discussion is also valuable as it helps to identify the problem and begins to address the reason behind it.

Discuss how they learn, and where something has worked reflect on it and try to help the child put into words what it was that he did. The value in this is firstly to make explicit the reasons for success and secondly to help the child to learn how he learns best.

Table 1.2 Assessment checklist

Assessment checklist	
1. Check basic mappings	• Letter-sound correspondences
2. Collect a core set of spelling data	• Spontaneous writing sample • Spelling list incorporating words of differing syllable length • Phonemically balanced regular word/non-word list
3. Categorize spelling errors	List all non-standard spellings and grade them according to how far they are away from the standard spelling: one easy means of doing this is to look at the word out of context and see how hard it is to decipher without clues as to its meaning. The more 'help' you need, the less phonemic referencing there is. • Standard spellings • Orthographic spellings • Phonemic spellings • Semi-phonemic spellings • Metaphonological • Non-phonemic Each of these categories reflects a particular level of dealing with phonological information, and thus can be very useful in determining the developmental status of the child's spelling patterns.
4. Look for patterns	Look for relationships among the data you have collected. Often as you look a pattern begins to emerge, and will provide clues as to the underlying nature of the spelling errors.
5. Prioritise your teaching objectives	Choose to start with those factors that are most disruptive to the child's ability to communicate his thoughts in writing.

Seeing change

How do you measure progress? It is often difficult to view progress if standardised assessments are the only measure used. Quantitative information – how many words are read or spelt correctly – is important, but when dealing with children who have significant and persisting difficulties, it can be of limited value. It is discouraging for both the pupil and the teacher if the score has not altered substantially, to reflect the amount of effort and work that has gone in from both sides. If a developmental approach is taken, small but significant qualitative changes can be appreciated and reflected.

This programme monitors how the child learns by looking at the developmental markers presented earlier; developmental progression and strategy use:

- phonemic segmentation span
- syllable length and complexity
- developmental strategy, error type, frequency and severity.

These measures are sensitive to small changes and are important for both the teacher and the child as both need to see and appreciate that progress is being made. The baseline measures gained from the initial assessment are entered onto the programme planner, and progress across all three dimensions can be effortlessly charted on a weekly basis.

Table 1.3 Assessment summary and teaching objectives/sequence for A.K.

Assessment summary		
Developmental		Descriptive
Strategy: Non-phonemic		Number of sound units the child can process: +/– 1
Major problem is the lack of basic letter-sound bonds, and the inconsistent nature of those he does have. His predominant strategy is the use of non-phonemic letter strings.		It is not possible to see any patterns beyond the emergence of occasional word initial phonemes. AK's data shows that he is not able in either reading or spelling to link sounds together. He is beginning to be able to process at the single sound level.
Summary: Severe phonological processing problems affecting auditory memory, sequencing and discrimination		
Prioritise teaching objectives		
1. Ensure that the mappings he has are well established so that we can begin to introduce some structural development – VC blending.	2. Introduce VC Synthesis/blending.	3. Work on establishing a full and consistent range of mappings to complete his inventory. Aim = 26/26
Teaching sequence		
(a) Present letters for him to read (recognition) and produce (retrieval). Those that he can use consistently for both functions can be considered as a 'working group'. Need to make sure that this group contains at least three short vowel sounds.	(a) Take 'working-group' sounds, and build a basic matrix. Use this to construct minimal pairs (pairs of words that differ by only one sound). (b) Collect pictures from magazines that show a variety of appliances, and use them to work on the terms 'on/off'. This can be done through both reading and spelling tasks. Any material can be used but it must conform to the two units of sound criterion.	(a) Because discrimination is a problem, start working on sounds that are dissimilar – belonging to different sound groups – to minimise confusion. (b) Use a contrastive approach. (c) When the letter-sound bond is established for both recognition and production, integrate it into the 'working group'.

Table 1.3 Continued

Assessment summary		
Developmental	Descriptive	
Summary of progress: Progress has been slow initially with VC synthesis proving difficult to establish, but the second half-term has seen some major developmental advances: 1. Almost complete inventory of sounds 22/26. Established for recognition and retrieval. 2. All working group sounds can be used in VC syllables, in reading and spelling of both words and non-words. 3. Have begun work on C-VC syllables and onset-rime strategies. 4. Have gone from +/– 1 sound units to 3. 5. As units of sound have increased, some patterns are beginning to emerge. If number of sounds exceeds three, there is a noticeable decline in accuracy – vowel transcription errors and final consonant voicing errors. Need to consolidate performance at this level. Extension testing should not be done until the end of term.		
Prioritise teaching objectives		
1. Give lots of practice and guided discovery exercises at the three sound unit level.	2. Aim to gradually increase the rate of presentation of stimuli.	3. Begin extension activities.
Teaching sequence		
Tasks should include sequencing, categorisation and discrimination, using word stimuli, and then if this goes well, non-word stimuli.	AK shows signs of phonemic instability and response latency effects if the stimulus words are presented at too high a rate. Need to ensure that he has sufficient processing time for each word.	Phrase level reading material; picture word matching etc.

Other factors are also important in the qualitative assessment of a child's progress:

- Timing, or automaticity – the time a child takes to complete a task can give a good indication of progress. When something new is introduced, it takes a lot of effort to process all the things you need to remember and apply to the task; as these are assimilated, the task becomes quicker.
- What needed to happen to help him reach the right response – did he need a lot of help or direction, or was his response quick and accurate?
- Did he talk himself through it, reminding himself of what he had learnt and applying it, did he give an immediate response that was incorrect and revise it, or did he need the error to be pointed out and was he then able to self-correct?
- How the child responds to the task/materials provided is a good indicator of progress and whether he feels he is making any. A favourite response at school is when the child gives a grin and says, 'I'm going to beat you at this today!' or 'Haven't you got anything harder? I can do this now.'

Table 1.3 shows AK's assessment summary and teaching objectives/sequence and demonstrates how the process follows through from initial assessment and setting teaching objectives to charting and monitoring progress.

Conclusion

Underlying both the assessment and treatment procedures are certain assumptions about the nature of a child's phonological system and the relationship between that system and the emergence of written language skills. The basic premise is that there is a strong and significant link between phonology and early reading and spelling, and that the phonological system is rule-governed and predictable. Any processing difficulties will manifest themselves in patterns and predictable ways in the 'visible phonology' of spelling.

> Thus, since rule-governed behaviour implies organisation, one's analysis should reveal the organisation which underlies the patterns, one's assessment should identify the deviations and inadequacies in the organisation, and one's treatment should be designed to change these deficient aspects of the organisation.
>
> (Grunwell 1985)

The emphasis of this programme is not on the symptoms – the spelling or reading errors themselves – but on the causes. It is hoped that by addressing these fundamental cognitive prerequisites, one can help the child to become more aware of his learning strengths and weaknesses, and introduce him to strategies and concepts that will provide a secure basis for further learning.

2 Syllables, segmentation, poetry and prose

Michael Thomson and Gill Gilmour

This chapter continues with the written language theme. The first and third parts look at the teaching of syllable and segmentation with some ideas and a description of a syllable analysis approach. In the second or middle section, Gill Gilmour shows how to bridge the gap between syllable and creative work by sharing her ideas on teaching poetry to dyslexics.

Phonological representation

The previous chapter has looked at the very basics of translating the spoken word into its written language equivalent. Speech input processes give rise to phonological representation, which is then translated into meaning or semantic representation and then the motor programming which could result in speech output or in writing. Another important stage in teaching is to develop these relationships further and this chapter looks at syllables and segmentation in particular. Initially, we will look briefly at some theoretical background information. Then we will look at how syllabification and awareness of written language structure can be aided by the use of poetry, and finally at some very specific examples of how to use syllable analysis to aid segmentation in teaching.

The phonological representation of words is affected by many different factors, including vocabulary size, the size and structure of the words themselves as well as their frequency, the particular language the person is using and the age of acquisition of words, as well as speech processes, reading and spelling acquisition. These are shown in Figure 2.1.

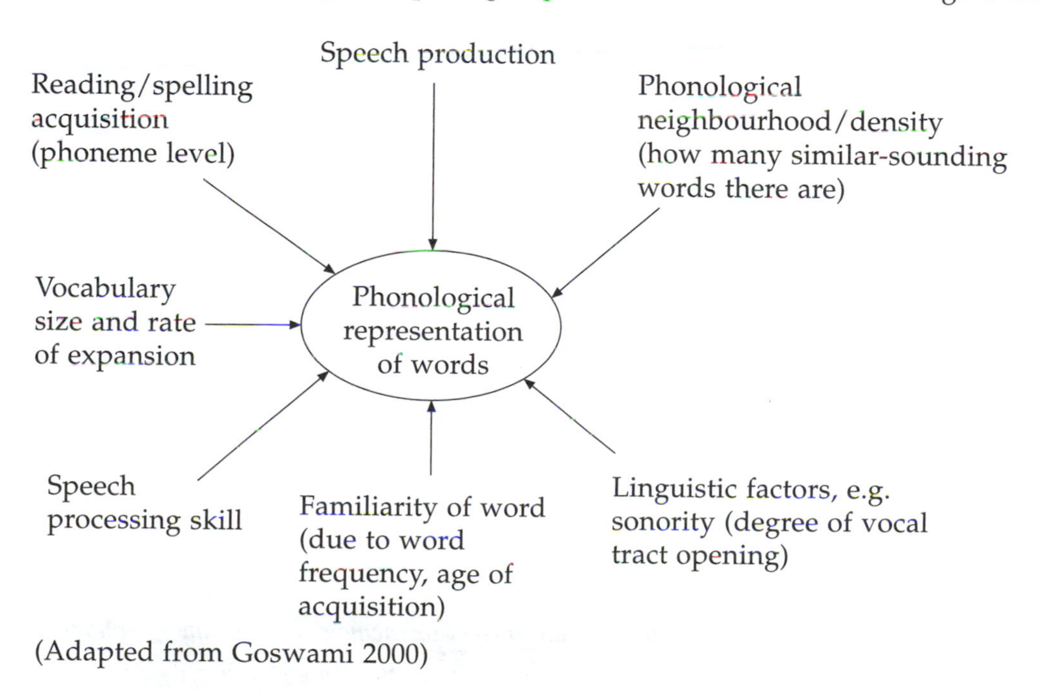

Figure 2.1 Factors affecting phonological representation

Here we intend to focus mainly on helping children to follow their own speech sounds and the use of segmentation and syllabification in aiding spelling and reading, as well as using word analysis skills to help the development of written language skills. Basic multi-sensory teaching involves integrating the visual/auditory and kinaesthetic and is the basis for teaching, for example, 'simultaneous oral spelling'. Here words are repeated, spelt out letter-by-letter, repeated again and written down with the words being said as they are traced or written, and finally read again.

Syllabification techniques aid phonological skills and these include segmentation, blending, rhyming and manipulation tasks at various levels. The child's phonological representations become increasingly segmented, according to Goswami (2000), as they begin to segment sounds within words, whether by syllables or individual phonemes. As vocabulary grows, the phonological representations are restructured so that smaller elements of sounds are represented. It is well established that the phonological representation of words, or a core phonological deficit, is a key factor in dyslexia. This is described elsewhere (e.g. Snowling 2000, Thomson 2001).

The ability to blend sounds together or to segment or separate sound units, and the use of alliteration and rhyming skills, are all good predictors of later reading skills. Phonemic ability, which again is associated with the relationship between speech and sound, and syllabification skills, sounding out words and separating them into sound units, are also important for word reading. There is an interaction here, i.e. the better you are at reading, the better you are at phonemic skills. Conversely, the better you are at phonemic skills, the better your reading is likely to be. This interrelationship is, of course, one of the problems in aspects of dyslexia research, particularly when looking at control groups. Phonemic ability, which to some extent is interactive, dependent on and gives rise to good word reading, is also linked to comprehension. Training, i.e. teaching by categorising sounds, phoneme discrimination and other such skills, can improve phonemic ability, which underlies both word reading and comprehension; this in turn can give rise to improved phonemic ability. It sounds rather complex and full of circularities, but it is important to understand this interactivity and 'networking' of the learning process.

Figure 2.2 illustrates various subdivisions/segments of words to help with terminology.

Let us move away from theoretical issues and consider teaching procedures.

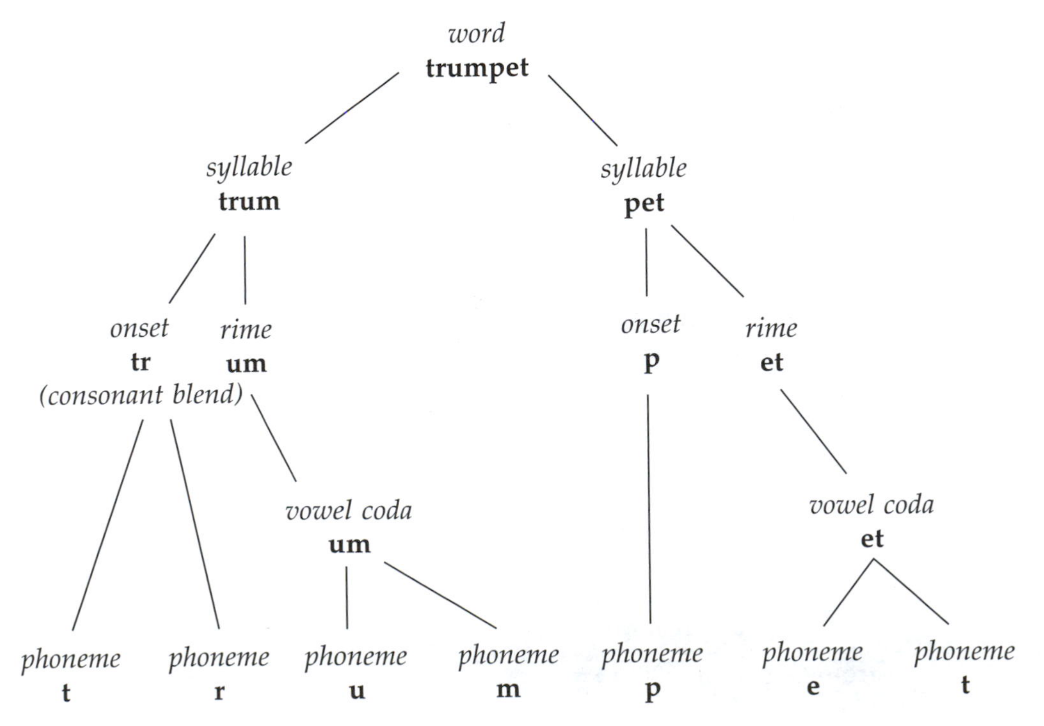

Figure 2.2 Possible linguistic subdivisions of 'trumpet'

1. Syllable monsters

The first stage obviously is to get children to become aware of following their own speech sounds and what a syllable is. We usually define this as a beat in a word and one useful way is starting with their own names and seeing if they can tap how many syllables are within that. A useful tip is also to ask a child to put the back of their hand underneath their chin and then they can say their name or appropriate words, and count how many times their chin goes down. You may like to try that for your own name and you will notice that every time your chin moves down onto your hand that is a syllable. We usually start off a class with general awareness of syllables and then find as many syllables as we can in words. Obviously this may be difficult for some children in terms of actually pronouncing words, such as deoxyribonucleic acid, but a lot of fun can be gained!

The next stage in awareness of syllables is to draw attention to various components of the syllable – that there must always be a vowel in the syllable, for example, and importantly that following syllables can aid spelling. The next stage would probably be the development of a 'syllable monster'. Here children would be encouraged to make up their own series of syllables, using real or non-word syllables, for example:

Pog / tag / rut / sop / lam / wot

The child is then asked to read that series of syllables back to the teacher or to the class, and then invited to draw a picture of the monster that those syllables represent. This could be an outlandish, weird fantasy creature, and then the child could be invited to colour it in. The picture could be accompanied by an account of what the monster does: for example, what the monster eats, where it lives, what noises it makes and its general habits. The pictures can then be put on the wall as a syllable zoo.

This seemingly silly task has a number of important functions. The first is to recognise that non-words can be read. This is a very important component of alphabetic skill development in children and is one of the key weaknesses that dyslexic children have. By introducing the reading of these non-words, it forces grapheme/phoneme correspondence without lexical access – the meaning of the word. This is an important skill to learn so that one can recognise new words and generalise. The other important feature is to recognise that complex and seemingly impossible long words can be built up from relatively short syllables and that each can be sounded out individually. One assumes that at this stage the children are reasonably fluent in CVC, CCVC, and even CCVCC units. Once the syllable monster has been created, one can have more fun with non-words, and the children can be ready to learn to read and spell regular words. This can start off with two, three or four-syllable words which are very constrained, something we shall look at later on in this chapter, but the next section is on further awareness of syllable work, which links to poetry.

Focusing on poetry allows the child to experiment with different kinds of syllable structures within words. However, it does have another important element – that of linking to composition and writing.

2. Poetry not prose

We all know that for many dyslexic children, having to produce written work is their greatest fear – they cannot spell, they find writing difficult, when stressed their mind goes blank, they panic and so on. So what do we do? We give them a large blank A4 sheet of paper, a pen and ask them to write a story. Maybe we give them much more guidance than that (which is even more to remember), but the whole experience becomes rather daunting. Of course, we use mind-mapping, linear planning and a whole host of other techniques to develop writing. These could form a book in themselves.

However, encouraging children to explore expressive writing through poetry allows them to express their ideas without the usual grammatical constrictions. It can also be very short and is normally drafted and redrafted, even by Poets Laureate, so the production of a fair copy is a reasonable expectation for everyone.

This is particularly important for dyslexic children, who often have a high level of creativity and good imagery but find it very difficult to express themselves verbally. To illustrate my suggestions I have included some examples of work written by children as a normal part of their class work.

The Office

The office is busy in every way,
Tapping computers continue all day.
People running around with coffee and tea,
The rattling of the janitorial key.
The stressful mumbling of the tensioned boss
Worried by last week's amazing loss.
The roar of the cleaner pushing a Hoover
Disturbing a meeting that is not yet over.

The office at night has a different sight,
Most of the people have gone for the night.
Coffee left there in the dark getting old,
The guard wandering round getting ever so cold.
In the morning the office again will be busy,
But for now the building is resting quite easy.

JG

It is possible for any child to produce this level of work. Obviously, there are many different ways, but here are some ideas which may help you plan your own routes.

One starting point in the first half-term for younger children who are learning about short vowels and CVC words for the first time is syllable poems. This is a good way to reinforce work done in phonics and link syllabification to creative writing.

A haiku is a Japanese form of poetry which has been adapted in many ways for use. The easiest to follow is to work towards a three-line poem with five syllables in the first line, seven syllables in the second line and five in the third. When the Japanese create these, they spend ages thinking, working and perfecting their ideas in much the same way as a diamond worker will study his stone for a long time before cutting and then there is still work to be done polishing for the jewel to be at its best. While this level of refinement is unnecessary for our purpose, there is often room for improvement.

The wind

The wind moves freely,
Never stops, just keeps going,
Passing on and on.

HN

Cinquains are found in several forms but it is useful to follow the syllable pattern 2, 4, 6, 8, 2, trying to make an impact in the last line.

Hunting

Hunting
The running fox.
The hunt comes thund'ring through
The wood, hounds eagerly chasing
To kill!

One form that may not be so familiar is the telephone poem, which can be fun to write. The number and length of lines to be used is determined by a telephone number, perhaps that of the school. The poem and the writing take the form of one half of a telephone conversation.

Hello, is that Natasha?
How was your holiday?
Wow!
Maybe I'll go there.
Yes! I hope so.
I'll try to see you at the weekend.

Back on more familiar ground there are acrostics, poems written by writing the title down the page and using those letters as the first or second letter of each line. It is often easier for children to start if they have a picture to help. These can be gathered from calendars, postcards, the Internet or, if desperate, bought. An acrostic also focuses on the phonemic level of word analysis, albeit always the initial sound and letter.

Lighthouse

Lonely in a field,
Isolated from all life.
Grass and flowers conceal small animals.
Helping sailors to pass safely
Through the rocky waters,
Hoping not to be betrayed.
Over the waves, the light swiftly flashes
Untangling sailors' troubles.
Surely boats go past the rocks,
Easily passing every time.

CG

Animals are a particularly good starting point with the advantage that the length of the poem is easily adjusted: 'Tiger' or 'Bengal tiger', 'Snake', 'Anaconda' or 'Boa constrictor'. For some children, knowing the precise route, seeing the end before they even start, is important – others do not seem to mind at all.

Moving away from syllabification and word analysis into poems in a more general sense of the word, there is usually an awareness of rhythm, the music of the poem. There are many good examples to be read: 'Tarantella' by Hilaire Belloc and 'Skimbleshanks' by TS Elliot are two that spring to mind.

One way to encourage writing is to take a topical theme which, regretfully, is nearly always tragic. Examples are Mozambique floods, Balkan wars, hurricanes and the destruction of the World Trade Center. You can encourage thoughtful, dramatic writing by asking the children to imagine that they are a press photographer taking a series of pictures for which they have to write captions. It is interesting to discover that many children will use assonance or alliteration spontaneously.

Flood

The rain was battering the roofs
Feeding the flood.
The constant flow forcing the people
To high places, safe places.
These havens will be engulfed soon.
The water rises like a hungry animal
Ferociously seeking the helpless humans,
The screams of children muffled to a mutter
By the dull clatter of helicopters taking pictures.
Not helping.
Taking pictures,
Not helping.

ST

Another important aspect of phonology is rhyme. Sometimes children ask about this and the reply is along the lines of 'Only if the poem wants to'. The music and the sense are more important. For many children, rhyme is an inhibitor or a problem due to phonological difficulties although many of you will use rhyming words to help with spelling (weak rhyming skills at four years old are a strong predictor of later written language difficulties in children). However, it can be encouraged if you so desire.

During a series of lessons for the oldest group planned to cover one and a half terms or three terms of alternate weeks, I decided to look at various rhyming forms. This began with nursery rhymes and working out the rhyme pattern.

Humpty Dumpty sat on a wall,	**A**
Humpty Dumpty had a great fall.	**A**
All the king's horses and all the king's men	**B**
Couldn't put Humpty together again.	**B**

We did this for several examples, which proved quite interesting because very few children seem to know the nursery rhymes today.

Initially, it was quite difficult to understand rhyme patterns but within a short time, not only did understanding come but also awareness of different types of rhyme such as 'again' and 'men' in Humpty Dumpty.

A rhyme was then written in the same session from a line worked out by the group, 'A boy was kicking a bouncy ball'. Do be careful about the rhyming word – another group chose 'A boy was running along a lane' which led to a lot of accidents involving a train.

From here we went to the ballad form. First I read a ballad to the group. We all have our favourites such as 'The Rime of the Ancient Mariner' or 'The Yarn of the Nancy Bell' which is suitably bloodthirsty.

Trying to produce a reasonably long ballad in a short time can be a problem and lends itself to group or joint writing, adding to work done by others. Alternatives that work well are calypso or raps.

February naturally requires some love poetry, Betjeman's 'A Subaltern's Love Song' or 'My love is like a red, red rose' by Burns, or poems dedicated to desirable objects rather than people. Then we wrote Valentines which provided a great opportunity for light-hearted or intensely emotional poems which most young writers enjoy.

'Will you marr-'
(The words get stuck in your throat.)
'Will you marri-'
(Oh heck, give me a break!)
'Will you marry me?'
You finally say
But the answer is 'No.'
Oh, oh, oh, oh.

To J____

As soft as a lamb,
As strong as a tree,
I love you,
I hope you love me.
I long for a loving hug,
I long for a kiss.
When you go away,
Your sweet presence I miss.

Our greatest challenge was the sonnet. I did not tell the group the form but read a selection and they worked out for themselves the number of lines, length of line, rhyming patterns, arrangements and the fact that the last six lines usually are from a different point of view. War poems such as Wilfred Owen's or sonnets by Keats are good. We aimed to get ten syllables to a line. Most reverted to rhyming couplets rather than more sophisticated patterns because they had so much to think about.

The last type considered was to write a poem on a subject about which one had strong feelings. I called these 'protest' poems although that is not strictly accurate. Having written a variety of poems, the students had the experience to choose their own form. This is where the depth and intensity of feeling becomes apparent. Poems that can bring lumps to your throat, poems that enable children to express fears and traumas or show incredible insight or self-awareness. This example is quite light-hearted but the writer really felt that he could not write poetry.

Bad Poetry

I can't write poems, I don't know why.
I start to write and I try
To come up with something clever.
But I don't think that I could ever.
My poems always turn out rubbish,
Not good enough to be published.
I find it hard to think what to say,
These things never go my way
And I cannot ever find a rhyme
For the very last line.

JG

Finally, it is important to remember the many opportunities that arise during the year for children to enter competitions. In most areas there are arts festivals which may have categories for original poems. This can give good feedback and the experience of performing. There are many similar opportunities and competitions that even allow children to have work selected for publication. The standard of work that is produced is quite surprising but, more importantly, it gives pleasure and satisfaction to the children who will often start to write poems purely for pleasure. Many of our poems have been published in Young Writers' 'Poetic Voyages'.

3. Syllable analysis

The poetry work relates syllable analysis to meaning and also introduces awareness of more complex structures such as rhyme. Parallel with such work (or earlier or later) children can move on to more systematic analysis skills. Earlier in the chapter it was mentioned that one can go on from syllable monsters to regular words; one technique might be to analyse a word such as 'cabinet'. Here children could put the numbers 1 to 3 across the top of the page and the word would be pronounced syllable by syllable: *cab – i – net*. At this stage the assumption is that the child can spell/read CVC or any word structures used. Children can then write the word syllable by syllable and then read the whole word. This can be built up by using four, five or even six-syllable words provided they are very carefully chosen to be regular or within the child's reading and spelling development within each syllable. Word lists with different levels and different kinds of syllables are given in Thomson and Watkins (1999). I quite like using long and unusual words for my older groups (i.e. 13 years), such as 'transmogrification', which has six syllables (although the *-tion* pattern would have to be taught beforehand), and longer words from the so-called 'impossible' word list, such as, 'anthropomorphic' and the like. What is important here is to have controlled word lists and examples available and also do some work on using nonsense words in a similar way to the syllable monsters outline.

The next stage is to begin to introduce syllable analysis by using six kinds of syllables. Broad details of this are given in Thomson and Watkins (*op. cit.*), while a definition of these is given in Table 2.1.

Table 2.1 Six types of syllables

Each syllable example is underlined. The key abbreviation for each is given in parentheses. (Note: the numbering of these after the first three is not crucial.)

Syllable type

1. The *open* syllable (o)

   me *no* *o*'pen *cry*'ing *fi*'nal

   The vowel is open at the end of the syllable; it is 'unprotected' and often says its long name; it is 'allowed' to as there are no consonants 'shutting it in'. In the 'cry' example 'y' is acting as a vowel.

2. The *closed* syllable (c)

   in *lost* o'*pen* cry'*ing* fi'*nal*

   The vowel is closed by one or more consonants; it is 'protected' and says its short sound; it cannot say its long name as it is 'shut in' – the consonant 'slams the door on it'; the closing in is after the vowel, not before it, thus *in* is closed.

3. The *VCE* or silent 'e' syllable (vce)

   ice *wine* *scrape* re'*bate* dis'*place*

   (suffix: drop 'e' – biting)
   The vowel has been opened by the silent 'e' and says its long name; the 'e' unlocks the door and allows the vowel to say its name.

4. The *R combination* syllable (rc)

   bird *ford* de'*ter*' mine *cur*'tain

   A vowel combines with the letter 'r'; the vowel comes first – ar, er, ir, or, ur. Not to be confused with a closed syllable. The important difference is the 'r'.

5. The *vowel combination* syllable (vc)

   wait *snow* *au*'gust *main'tain* de'*stroy*'ing

   Here, one of the vowel combinations forms the syllable – see text for discussion of what constitutes a vowel combination.

6. The *-le* or *consonant -le* syllable (-le)

   ta'*ble* pad'*dle* stee'*ple*
   (suffix: drop 'e' – strug'gl'ing)

   A consonant occurs before the -le, -ble, -ple etc., the 'l' sound is thus spelt -le with a consonant in front of it.

An example of words divided into syllables and analysed could be:

o rc a'corn	vc c spoon'ful'	o rc c vce re'or'gan'ise
c rc o c trans' for'ma'tion	c vce stag'nate	c - le crum'ble

Note that the words are divided with the syllable type on the top.

Note that we use the following conventions: we refer to 'long name' for vowel sound as 'o' in 'no' and 'short sound' for vowels as 'o' in 'not'.

Vowel combinations could be: vowel digraphs, – e.g. 'maid'; diphthongs, e.g. 'boil'; or letter combinations that include consonants but are vowel sounds, e.g. 'might'. We teach (ā), (ē), (ī), (ō), (ū), as well as (ow) in cow or round, (or) in automatic and (oy) in boil or boy, in other words, a total of eight 'vowel combinations'.

Most of the English language can be divided into the six kinds of syllables and it is very useful for children to use these in analysing words in reading and for spelling. This not only gives children useful skills which are very important for their written language development, but also does give them some special knowledge which they have over other children or even teachers who are not privy to this word analysis skill. The focus is often on vowel sounds, but not always. We usually start with open and closed syllables with the younger children. As shown in Table 2.1, this focuses on the vowel being shut in, and again one can start with carefully selected words, for example, with flash cards, in spelling or even reading them out from text. Here are some examples of two-syllable words with controlled syllable types.

1 closed syllable only	2 closed and open syllable	3 closed, open and vce syllable
kidnap	duet	inside
problem	student	confuse
humbug	final	tadpole
cutlass	dial	bagpipe
velvet	gravy	produce

As one goes along in presenting words on flash cards or for spelling, one can gradually increase the syllable numbers and introduce different types of syllables and, again, word lists for this purpose are given in Thomson and Watkins (*op. cit.*). Once the syllable analysis system has been learnt by the teacher initially and then taught and learnt by the child, it is used in many different ways, such as the following:

1. Writing words on the board or from a book; the children can write them down, divide them into syllables and into syllable types, as per the examples given in Table 2.2.

Table 2.2 Some examples of syllable analysis

magnet	c mag	c net			
tadpole	c tad	vce pole			
table	o ta	-le -ble			
toem	o po	c em			
magnificent	c mag	c nif	o i	c cent	
destroyer	c des	vc troy	rc er		
mountain	vc moun	vc tain			
reincarnation	o re	c in	rc car	o na	c tion

Note that	o de	vc stroy	rc er	would be acceptable.

2. Coming across new or difficult multi-syllable words, dividing them into syllables, looking at possible pronunciations of the words, depending upon what kind of syllable type is used; for example a two-syllable word like 'lady' could be *la – dy* or *lad – y*, although in the former case the vowel would be long, as it is an open syllable and this would be the correct pronunciation, whereas in the second case the vowel would be

short and would lead to incorrect pronunciation. These possible word pronunciations could be compared with other real words and also aid vocabulary development.

3. Controlled word lists of particular syllable types can be used for reading and then subsequent analysis into syllables, as in 1 above.
4. Syllable analysis can be used in particular to draw distinctions between the different vowel structures that we have in English. For example, words such as 'boiling,' where the *oi* is a vowel combination of a particular sound, can be contrasted with 'idiot', where the *io* juxtaposition is not a vowel combination in the sense that it does not make one sound. I have found this very useful for words where there are different vowel combinations to help to decide when you split between two vowels and when you do not.
5. It encourages children to follow their own speech sounds in syllable work, and by making them analyse the syllables, makes them focus much more attention upon the written language structure, which is useful for building up phonological representations of words – which is where we came in at the beginning of the chapter.
6. Discussions about word structure – not every word analysis will be agreed on (see destroyer above) and interesting arguments can be had!

Finally, I would like to comment that we carried out some research in the school a few years ago on syllable analysis. Children were invited to spell two or three-syllable words in a pre-test, and then they were given syllable analysis training where they divided words into their syllable units and gave them as syllable types, as described here. Another group was asked to look, to copy out and to read the whole word. Those who did syllable analysis made much greater improvement than those who just copied out the word. The results are shown in Figure 2.3.

Control group: look, say, copy, read (dyslexic non-treatment) ....
Treatment group: divide into beat, analyse, write down (dyslexic) ________

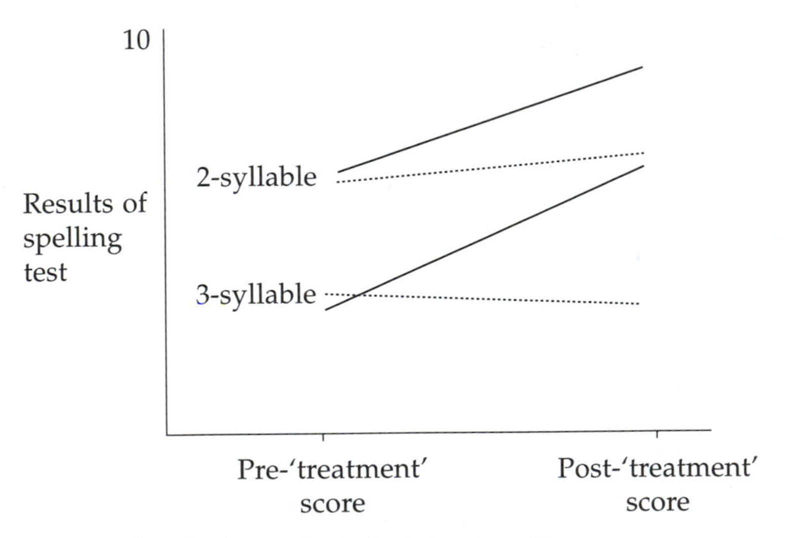

Figure 2.3 Effects of syllable analysis training teaching

Although this was a very small-scale study carried out over a short period of time (we did not want to deprive the other children of carrying out syllable work, which we felt was helpful), nevertheless the result was encouraging, as the 'syllable analysis' group made good progress whereas the control group made no progress.

3 Dyslexia and Mathematics

John Weavers

It is now recognised that many dyslexics have difficulties in aspects of mathematics. Here John Weavers shares his observations on the sorts of difficulties facing dyslexics, including the language of mathematics. Learning styles and approaches to teaching are discussed, with examples.

It is estimated from initial research carried out by Joffe (1983), Henderson (1998) and Miles and Miles (2002) that up to 60 per cent of dyslexic children will also have difficulties in understanding mathematical concepts and learning computational skills to a greater or lesser degree.

The term 'dyscalculia' is often used to describe this condition, which affects the child's ability to grasp computational skills and, despite normal intelligence, will create difficulties in reasoning and the understanding of the basic mathematical concepts. I will use the term as a shorthand for the varied arithmetical, mathematical and computational problems associated with dyslexia, which are described below. Although dyscalculia can occur independently from dyslexic difficulties, our experience is of a large overlap. We too find approximately 60 per cent of our children have difficulties in mathematics.

Mathematics is a subject of great diversity, covering topics of size, time, shape and space; however, all the facets of the subject require a sound foundation of basic arithmetical skills. A lack of these skills is not only going to hinder one's progress in this subject alone but also in all other areas of the curriculum. It will be a hindrance to personal progress and an embarrassment in adult life. Facing up to the problem is essential, for with understanding and with good teaching, a lot can be achieved. We should no longer accept the statement from personalities in the public eye, 'Well, I was never much good at maths when I was at school', as if it were 'not cool' to be too good at the subject.

Understanding the problem

It is generally accepted that many of the underlying cognitive difficulties that affect a child with dyslexia will also be the core factors affecting their progress in mathematics.

These difficulties can be classified as follows. I list them briefly below and shall then consider each in greater detail, so that a clearer knowledge and better understanding of these factors will help us to empathise with the difficulties faced by a child with dyscalculia, and subsequently enable us to offer help more sympathetically and more successfully.

- Maths is a new language to many children, with new words, signs and symbols to be learnt. There is a lot of duplication and ambiguity of meaning to come to terms with at all levels. For a child with a low reading ability, the prospect can be daunting.
- Left-right orientation weaknesses may cause difficulties – having been struggling to read from left to right, children are suddenly confronted with working down the page in columns, or from right to left.
- Sequencing and logical progression when looking for patterns and procedures for

setting out work is often weak, especially when one considers that maths requires a lot of abstract thinking, and putting it down on paper is difficult.

- Short-term and working memory difficulties are a problem for most, if not all, dyslexic children. Maths is a subject that relies heavily on previously learnt work before progression to the next step is undertaken. This tiered approach is a major problem for those with a poor memory. Many pupils will also copy incorrectly, or forget the end objective of a problem being tackled.
- Long-term memory (or possibly transfer from working memory into long-term memory) is a handicap in many areas of the subject, whether it be the inability to learn one's number bonds and master the multiplication tables, or the inability to remember formulae required for more complex work.
- Slow processing speed: not only may a child be inherently working at a slower pace, and needing more practice and reinforcement, but the speed of the lesson designed for the non-dyslexic will leave him further behind, thus compounding the problem.
- Poor spatial awareness and perceptual skills: difficulty will be experienced in interpreting diagrams and charts correctly, or problems will be experienced when filling in data or copying from the board or another page. Signs and symbols will be confused and misinterpreted.
- Weak conceptual ability: mathematics is best learnt by understanding concepts – why we do certain things in a certain way. This knowledge is often weak in the case of a dyslexic child, who may be reinforcing his skills through repetition and drill, thus limiting his experiences and understanding.
- A clash of mathematical learning profiles: mathematics can be tackled and understood in different ways. It is particularly important with dyslexic children that the teacher or tutor recognises his or her own cognitive learning style, i.e. whether he or she has developed his or her knowledge of the subject through rote or conceptual understanding. Different children will succeed in different ways, and it is important that a tutor teaches to suit the learning profile of the child.

Now let us consider in greater depth each of these potential areas of difficulty, so that we can begin to understand a little more fully the nature of the problems encountered. By so doing we can thus develop strategies that will go some way in helping to alleviate the problems faced by a dyslexic child while trying to cope with this subject.

The language of mathematics

It is clearly acknowledged that mathematics is indeed a new language to all children. There are numerous mathematically specific words to learn and understand. There are signs, symbols and abbreviations to come to terms with and formulae to comprehend. We must not assume that even the good reader will have no problems in reading and understanding mathematical text. The text may not always be as clear and simple as it could be; many of the words will be new to the children; and there will be considerable ambiguity or duplication of meaning. Many words or symbols can be used to mean the same thing, or one word could in itself have many meanings. A child whose mathematical capabilities and potential might be of a good standard may well have their confidence and self-esteem shattered at this stage. They will need a lot of guidance, support and understanding to overcome this major hurdle of language, or the result will be increased frustration and despair and any early success will be lost. It is interesting to note that research into mathematical attainment in other countries shows that where the mathematical language is simple and less ambiguous (e.g. Japan), the level of children's attainment can be advanced by over a year. It is important that we reduce the problem of language as much as possible at its source. A child may be receiving mathematical language input from a variety of different sources, as Figure 3.1 shows.

Our first priority is that of continuity. We must endeavour to formulate between these factions a common level of mathematical vocabulary to suit the attainment level of the child. This is particularly important between teachers, classroom assistants and hopefully parents; continuity should be the same within parallel classes and should develop in

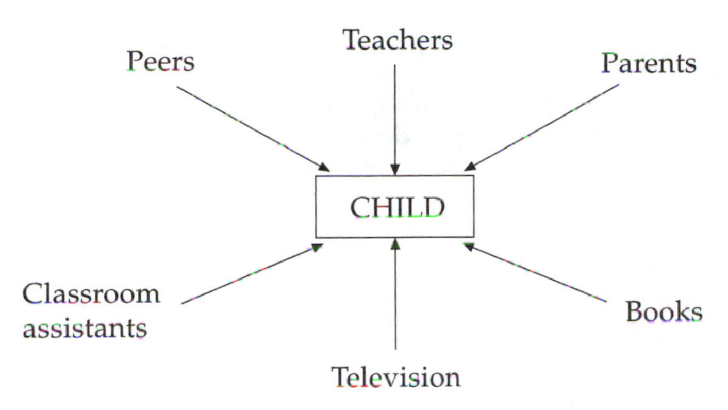

Figure 3.1 Sources of mathematical language

phases as the child progresses through the school. We will look again at this background of continuity of approach to avoid confusion, for it is important that we all adopt the same techniques for arithmetical layout and calculation and, to a lesser degree, problem solving.

Let us consider the basic symbols, terms and phrases that confront a child, and let us not assume that they will automatically link them together, for there are often many expressions that all have the same meaning.

- $+$ add, total, sum of, plus, and, altogether, addition, more than, positive
- $-$ subtract, take away, minus, difference between, less, smaller than, negative
- $\times$ (often confused with +) times, multiply, product of, lots of
- $\div$ divide, share, how many in, how much each, quotient
- $=$ equals, becomes, is the same as, makes
- $>$ greater than, often confused with $<$ less than

To overcome this overload of input it is advisable, wherever possible, to introduce only a few words at a time until they have been learnt and their meanings understood. The latter is particularly important; for example, the use of the word 'times' will result in one of two calculations depending on its context in the sentence. For example (i) 'What is 15 times 3?' or (ii) 'How many times does 3 go into 15?' When used in the context of a problem, it can be even more confusing, e.g. 'Dad is 40, his son is 8, how many times older is the father?' Obviously not 320, yet a child who has become 'command specific' when seeing the word 'times' will indeed 'times' 40 and 8. It all boils down to understanding the meaning of the sentence. (It does not help either that 'Dad' has been replaced with the word 'father' within the sentence.) We must of course encourage pupils to ask themselves, 'Is my answer sensible?' thus linking understanding with the idea of estimation and approximation at an early stage.

Another common source of error and misunderstanding that we need to be aware of is the use of the word 'more'. For example (i) 'What is 10 more than 50?' or (ii) 'How many more than 10 is 50?' One question implies addition, the other subtraction. To add even further confusion we might even ask the question, 'How many times more is 50 than 10?' and we begin to get an idea of the frustration and despair felt by many of our dyslexic children.

One strategy that does seem to help many children when faced with such questions is to get them to ask themselves the question, 'Do I expect the answer to be bigger or smaller than what I started with?' If they can answer this question correctly it will help their progress by narrowing the procedure down to a possible +, ×, or –, ÷ response, from whence a little careful reasoning will help them to make the correct choice. We must carefully cultivate this idea of a 'reasoned response' against the notion of a 'word command'.

The notion of size and value is often a difficult concept for some of our children to grasp, for we use the ambiguous words 'bigger' and 'smaller' to express both of these meanings. This is clearly illustrated by asking the question, 'Which is the bigger number, 5 or 3?' Do we mean bigger in size or value?

Later in their schooling, confusion persists when we consider decimals and place value, e.g. (i) 'Which is bigger, 5.3 or 35?' or (ii) '1.35 or 35?'

There are numerous examples of ambiguity in the English language that affect the young mathematician, thus causing understandable confusion and anxiety. Take, for example, the word 'volume'. We might be referring to the volume of a box or a room, or to the volume being too loud on their CD player. We might ask a noisy group to 'keep the volume down'. Another example would be in the use of the word 'face'. We talk of someone having a dirty face, and we tell them to face the front and look at the face of the clock, or to count the faces on a tetrahedron. For many children it is expecting a lot of them not to show some confusion!

Confusion is compounded when we consider that in addition to decoding the meaning of words in the correct context, and decoding symbols, we then introduce abbreviations for children to grapple with. These have to be decoded and then understood. Take, as an example, Lowest Common Multiple (LCM) and Highest Common Factor (HCF). Firstly, a child has to remember what each letter stands for; secondly, understand the meaning of each word; and thirdly, the meaning of the phrase. If we were to ask a pupil for the LCM of 12 and 15, further confusion arises, because the first word 'lowest' forms a mental image of something small – they anticipate a small answer and often the meaning of 'multiple' is overlooked as it is at the end, consequently we get the wrong answer 3. The same applies with HCF; 'highest' triggers off a big answer image and we are given the answer 60, the words 'multiple' and 'factor' being overlooked and confused. Perhaps it would be kinder to reverse the letters and ask for the MCL or the FCH so that the first mental image would focus on the words 'multiple' and 'factor'. The thought process would then be, 'I want a multiple that is common to both and is the lowest possible' and we arrive at the correct answer 60. Similarly, I want a factor common to both that is the highest possible.

Another example of the reversing of information that causes major problems is the way in which we tell the time. If we were all consistent in the way we interpreted a clock face, the problem would be greatly reduced, but when the time is 2:40 how many of us say '20 to 3'?

So the child with dyscalculia is faced with the problem of maths being a new language before he even thinks about solving problems and doing sums (note that the word 'sum' is also used to mean addition).

Our first task is to ensure that we know the reading ability of the pupils in our care, and target written work and questions at the correct level. Questions should not be excessively long, as a child with a combined poor memory and low reading score will have forgotten the beginning of the sentence before he reaches the end. Secondly, we must avoid overloading by not introducing too many new signs, symbols, abbreviations, words and phrases in one go, particularly those with ambiguous meanings. The introduction of the metric system in itself may be simple to understand and manipulate, but only after a vast number of similar sounding words have been learnt. To make matters doubly difficult, we are still operating a dual system with 'pints' being sold, and signposts giving distances in miles. If you ask children themselves how tall they are and how much they weigh, nine out of ten will give you a reply in feet and inches, and stones and pounds. We need to help children to become familiar with this new mathematical language by highlighting or underlining the important new words to be learnt as they appear in text. Their correct meanings can be compiled, which can then be easily discussed and referred to, thus reinforcing understanding and spelling.

Being aware of the confusion with language faced by a dyslexic child trying to cope with mathematics is the first step forward in giving him the chance to succeed in this subject.

Left-right orientation

Dyslexics frequently experience difficulties with left-right orientation and spatial awareness when setting out work, performing calculations and initially when writing numbers.

For children with directional difficulties, problems are compounded when we consider that they are being taught to scan from left to right across the page when learning to read. Numbers, when written down, follow the same direction, left to right, yet when we start to tackle simple arithmetic we introduce working down the page in columns for the first time, and reverse the left to right direction when adding, subtracting and multiplying. Starting at the right with our initial calculation, we move backwards to the left as we proceed to work out our answer, yet we must not forget that as children move on to learn division we reverse this process and start our calculation at the left and proceed to the right. Little wonder that further confusion results, for when adding, subtracting and multiplying, we have proceeded from right to left during calculation but when we read back our answer, we read from left to right. It is not surprising, therefore, that often we see the number one hundred and twenty-three written as 321.

The reading and writing of larger numbers is frequently an even greater problem for children with directional difficulties. Take, as an example, the number 1234567. It is not possible to read this number from left to right and give a value to it until we have firstly split it up into how many hundreds, tens and units there are, how many thousands there are, and how many millions. This, of course, requires us to start at the right of the number and move backwards to the left, blocking the digits into groups of three, before we can proceed to read the number correctly from left to right. Naturally this skill is made more difficult when we introduce the decimal point and have to consider place value more carefully. The use of squared paper at this stage will greatly assist, both with neatness of presentation and correct layout, particularly when the decimal point is introduced into calculations and correct place value has to be mastered.

One final aspect to consider is the order or sequence in which numbers occur in a question from left to right. For example, if we take the question 29 – 16 nearly all children would write down the 29 first followed by the 16 underneath, and continue with their subtraction. If the question were worded 'From 29 take away 16' the same process and result would be achieved. But if the 16 were to occur first in the sentence as it is read from left to right, for example 'Take 16 away from 29', a good proportion of children would incorrectly set out their sum as $\begin{array}{r}16\ -\\ \underline{29}\end{array}$ indicating both a fixation for copying things down as they appear in a sentence, and a lack of conceptual understanding which I shall consider again later.

Problems with sequencing

It is well understood and acknowledged that most dyslexic children are poor at following procedures and arranging in order events, words, symbols and series of numbers. Some find it difficult to arrange in order the events in their day, even when asked to do so verbally, or to arrange in order a series of pictures. Many have a similar problem with the seasons of the year, finding it difficult to relate weather, temperature, daylight hours, the birth of young animals, leaf cover and colour changes. Remembering sequences, following instructions and pattern recognition can be a major problem.

Most of the mathematics that is taught in schools, by the very nature of the subject, is taught sequentially. The order in which topics can be tackled is in itself restricted to a sequence of understanding and comprehension. Let us take as an example 'percentages'. To tackle percentages we need to have an understanding of fractions; to tackle fractions, a knowledge of multiples and factors is needed in addition to having a working understanding of one's multiplication tables; and all this in turn hinges upon having mastered successfully the algorithms of add, subtract, multiply and divide.

Individual topics within the subject rely heavily upon the ability to follow a sequence or order of progression. When teaching the area of compound shapes, for example, if we set the question 'Find the area of:'

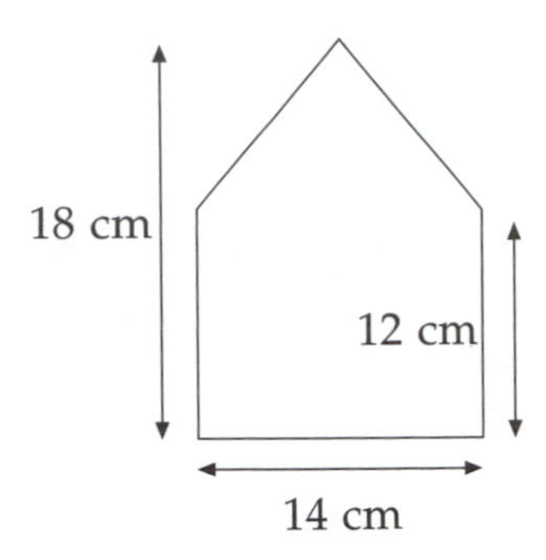

we might expect the following sequence to be followed:

1. Copy down the diagram in pencil.
2. Write in the values.
3. Split up the diagram into its component shapes.
4. Write down the formulae you intend to use.
5. Calculate any additional dimensions needed.
6. Substitute into the correct formula.
7. Calculate area of rectangle – show all working.
8. Calculate area of triangle – show all working.
9. Combine correctly the two answers calculated.
10. Put in the correct units (cm^2) and underline.

This approach, although important, may not be the easiest way forward for the dyslexic student who is far more likely to show a reluctance for working on paper, preferring to work in his head and jotting down salient data as the problem unfolds.

At an earlier stage the basic skills required to master the four rules of number: +, −, ×, ÷, all rely heavily on the ability to follow a set sequence. One has to consider many factors, and in the correct order. These may include:

1. Correct setting out.
2. Largest number on top when subtracting and multiplying.
3. Do you start at the left or the right?
4. Do you need to 'borrow' when subtracting?
5. When do you put down the extra 0 in long multiplication?
6. Do not forget to put carrying figures down in the correct place.
7. Do not forget to include any carrying figures in the next step.
8. Add up both lines when long multiplying.

The inclusion of the decimal point and the importance of correct place value, at a later phase, naturally put even greater demands on many of our dyslexic pupils.

Many of our pupils find it difficult to recognise a sequence, whether it be moving backwards or forwards by a multiple of ten, or a simple arithmetic progression such as 3, 6, 9, 12 etc. Time needs to be spent in helping children to master the ability to count in ones, twos, fives and tens, thus providing the foundation for the learning of their tables. This will also help them at an early stage to understand the importance of order and sequence. Ultimately, although a lot more difficult for some, they should be encouraged to reverse the sequence and count backwards. This ability naturally leads at a later stage to the understanding and concept of negative numbers, when one counts backwards through zero. This concept of negative values is made easier for pupils to accept if concrete examples of temperatures below freezing or bank balances 'in the red' are introduced and discussed. As always, a visual image or concrete example to hang new mathematics learning on should greatly facilitate progress.

Short-term and working memory

The short-term memory problems faced by our dyslexic children are without doubt a major factor hindering their progress in mathematics. Maths, by its very nature, relies heavily upon previously learnt knowledge and information, and any child who has difficulty in retaining information from week to week, or from lesson to lesson, will be at a great disadvantage. Techniques for the setting out of work and the procedures involved in even the simplest of calculations will be forgotten, facts will be lost and formulae remembered incorrectly, if at all. Dyslexic children often have difficulty putting a meaning to the symbols they are constantly confronted with in this subject; their attention span is low and they are slower and less well organised in general during lessons. It is therefore essential that a far greater emphasis is placed upon ensuring that they understand what is being taught and that they comprehend why calculations are tackled in a particular way, and how any formulae used are derived. A child will go further in this subject and have a good proportion of his short-term memory problems reduced if underlying mathematical concepts are understood as they are being taught. Learning by rote suits very few in this subject as it relies too heavily on one's memory skills. I shall deal with this more fully in a later section.

Constant reinforcing, with emphasis being placed upon understanding, is therefore the best solution for achieving success and helping the dyslexic child to transfer knowledge, skills and information from short-term to long-term memory.

A carefully structured approach is therefore important, and any haphazard bombarding of too much information too quickly will only result in overload and disaster.

A lot of our children, because of their dyslexia, also have a poor 'working memory' and this, combined with a low reading attainment, compounds their problems when reading a question, understanding instructions and arriving at an answer. They may indeed struggle through the reading of a question, and by the time they reach the end they will have forgotten the beginning; or they may in the end successfully read a sentence but not be able to give any understanding or meaning to it. Often, when a question is in a number of parts or requires a number of stages of calculations to arrive at the answer, they may lose sight of their goal and finish halfway through, forgetting what their original objective was. This is hardly surprising considering one of the many tests for dyslexia is 'digit span' analysis, i.e. the ability to repeat or even copy down a series of numbers correctly, a skill inherently poor in children with dyslexia. Deficits in short-term memory are therefore a major problem. Only by teaching slowly, and consistently reinforcing and focusing on understanding, can we go some way to finding a solution. Facts, details and methods of calculation, and to some extent the multiplication tables, may then have a greater chance of finding a more permanent home in a child's long-term memory.

Long-term memory

The nature of dyslexia and its associated problems has meant that it is only through a conceptual understanding of what is being taught that a child will have any real chance of retaining information, facts, formulae, algorithms or data over the long term. For the dyslexic, learning by rote as a means of assimilating information into the long-term memory will be a frustrating and demoralising experience, and although many teachers and parents will persist in trying to teach in this manner it is rarely effective, often resulting in considerable anxiety about the subject and a sense of failure. The learning of multiplication tables by rote for the dyslexic is a prime example of a lot of effort and time being expended for a limited amount of success. The National Numeracy Strategy accepts that within any group of children there will be a diverse set of abilities and learning styles, and that many different methods and strategies for arriving at an answer will be employed. It is in the light of this accepted individuality that we must encourage any strategy that works in the quest to learn one's multiplication tables.

Verbal association is difficult and learning by rote even harder for the dyslexic, as memory fails them time and time again. Possibly the best approach in our quest for success is a combination of strategies dependent upon the individual child and the multiplication table in question. A good proportion of dyslexic children do indeed manage to master their 'twos', (thus discovering odd and even numbers), their 'fives' and their ten times tables by rote learning; some go on to master more. The approach best suited to achieving this is a multi-sensory one. The table in question is clearly printed out in full in large font and is on the table in front of them. A 'look, touch, hear and say' approach should be employed and regular repetition and reinforcement may lead to success for some of our pupils with some of their tables. The child should run his finger along the table as he reads out the table in question, reinforced by the voice of a helper or a tape. Let us not feel embarrassed about chanting our tables; we have passed through the era when it was considered not to be 'the done thing'. The fact is it does help many of our pupils, but not necessarily all of them, in which case other tried and tested strategies have to be adopted.

We have a policy at East Court that all children have easy access to a 'table square', which is a grid of answers for any multiplication of two numbers up to ten. The child finds the two numbers to be multiplied, one in the vertical column on the left, the other in the row across the top. Where the column and row intersect is the correct answer. A table square is invaluable for providing the correct answer, and for allowing a child to progress at a steady pace through their work without getting lost and losing sight of their objective, while struggling to find out what 6 × 9 is, for example. It allows pupils to progress onto further maths even though they may still be having difficulties with simple arithmetic. Confidence as a result is boosted, for we are permitting children to use their intelligence at problem solving and not allowing them to become totally disenchanted as they continue to flounder with simple arithmetic as a result of memory problems. It could be argued that if a calculator is available the result would be the same; to some degree this is true, but a calculator is not always at hand in day-to-day life, at the shops or travelling in a car, for example. Far too often a calculator is incorrectly programmed, yet a child will insist the answer must be right because a calculator has been used. This is a further good example for encouraging a pupil to estimate their answer before any work is started, and at the end to ask themselves, 'Is my answer sensible?'

Another objective in placing higher emphasis on the use of a table square is that in addition to providing the correct answer, patterns and sequences of numbers will be discovered and on closer inspection these form a valuable foundation for developing other strategies in helping children to cope with their tables. The importance of the diagonal line of 2 × 2, 3 × 3, 4 × 4, 5 × 5, 6 × 6 etc. should be stressed and the notion of square numbers thus introduced; every effort should be made to learn these by heart, perhaps with the help of simple rhymes or chants. It should also be pointed out at an early stage that the numbers are reversible (the commutative law) 3 × 4 is the same as 4 × 3; sometimes one way will trigger the correct answer when the other leaves a blank. Many of our pupils, as a result of their dyslexia, develop strong reasoning powers and discover compensatory strategies which help them to overcome their inability to learn their tables by rote. Although the search for the correct answer takes longer, any strategy that works should be encouraged. This may well include extensive use of their fingers as they count on in groups of twos, threes or fours, and obvious patterns as in the five times table should be noted. It should be pointed out that any number multiplied by 4 is the same as that number being multiplied by 2 and then doubled, so for example 4 × 7 = 7 × 4 = 7 × 2 × 2. Another technique is to go for the nearest known answer and then to step count up or down till the correct answer is achieved. For example, 6 × 7 might be achieved by knowing that 6 × 7 = 7 × 6 and that 6 × 6 = 36, then 7 × 6 = 36 add another 6. Alternatively, it might be calculated via the route 6 × 5 or 5 × 6 are 30 add on 6, add on another 6. 8 × 3 might be obtained from 10 × 3 = 30 take away 3, take away 3. Any number multiplied by 9 can be reached by multiplying by 10 then subtracting the required number, e.g. 7 × 9 = 7 × 10 minus 7. Many children are encouraged to use the simple trick of using their fingers for their nine times table. The hands are placed flat on the table; if the answer to 4 × 9 is wanted, the fourth finger counting from the left remains on the table and all other fingers, including thumbs, are raised. The answer is the three fingers to the left of the finger on the table, combined with the fingers to the right of the finger still on the table (i.e. six), therefore 4 × 9 or 9 × 4 = 36.

There are many strategies that can be employed, but it soon becomes evident that no one method will bring success on its own. It is therefore necessary to adopt a flexible approach to the teaching of tables. A combination of rhymes, skills, tricks and strategies, and the drawing upon a dyslexic child's enhanced powers of reasoning will all lead towards a good degree of success. As always, it is important that the teaching given should suit an individual's cognitive learning style, which I shall refer to again in a later section.

Slow processing of information

The National Numeracy Strategy designed to promote the teaching of mathematics has many implications that affect children with a problem in this subject. One potential difficulty is the emphasis placed upon working accurately at speed and completing given tasks within a set time span. The dyslexic child's lack of automaticity and poor ability to recall facts and information in an instant leaves him at a considerable disadvantage, particularly if in a mixed ability classroom. The inability to rote learn facts, number bonds and tables is highly likely to occur and this, in addition to the problems of language reading and comprehension, leaves the dyslexic child struggling in the classroom. When he needs *more* time to process and complete work, in addition to practising it and reinforcing it, in fact he gets *less* than his non-dyslexic peers. He can easily find himself in a perpetual downward spiralling 'catch-up' situation. If put under this pressure of restricted time, progressing too quickly to assimilate new work and having no possibility of essential reinforcement, a child will soon become anxious and demoralised. He is racing to keep pace. Focus, accuracy and understanding fade; his inherent problems of poor copying skills from the board or book are exaggerated. Under this pressure he may miss out sections or mix up lines, copying part of one with part of another. He is certain to reverse numbers, copy them incorrectly or leave some out completely. Confidence will be shattered, he will arrive home with homework to complete: 'Finish off what you failed to complete in class then go on to exercise 5c.' Not only will he subsequently have more to do than his classmates, he will also have to complete it employing his inherently slower information processing skills, perhaps spending, in the end, twice as long on it as his peers. Such a scenario reinforces how important it is to identify children who find themselves in this frustrating situation and how important it is that they receive specialist help and then continue to work at a pace that suits their ability and addresses their special needs.

Poor visual perception skills

A small proportion of dyslexic children see things differently from their peers or tutors. They have weak perception skills and may not be able to interpret graphs, charts, patterns and diagrams presented to them in the way intended by their teachers. In the very early stages of learning the subject, these may be the same children who confuse sixes and nines or threes and fives and constantly mix up + and ×, not seeing them as being different. They will have great difficulty consequently when copying from the board or another book, constantly losing their place and making errors. These same children may also have difficulty with the harsh contrast of black ink on white paper. The solution for some, in reducing what is described as a 'shimmering, wobbly' effect, is the use of transparent coloured overlays to reduce the overall glare; while others gain relief by not sitting in bright light or in direct sunshine when reading. When using a computer, the simple solution is to change the print colour or background colour or simply to turn down the contrast. This is a problem not just confined to mathematics, as visual perception difficulties affect all subjects. In addition to highly contrasting text, particular problems arise in areas where coloured maps, charts and diagrams are used, as in geography, statistics and science. The interpretation of maps, outlines, block graphs and scientific diagrams for some dyslexic pupils can be most confusing. The interpretation of a 3D object represented on a flat piece of paper is beyond some of our pupils; they will continue to see a diagram, no matter how many ways it is hatched or shaded, as simply a collection of lines meeting at different angles. In maths, a two-dimensional sketch of a cube may be interpreted as just a square with two attached parallelograms, or in a scientific experiment they may draw a tripod as a triangle with three radiating lines, one from each corner. To help children with such difficulties, they must have the opportunity to play with building bricks and blocks of all shapes and sizes, and apparatus and concrete models should be available in the classroom for them to see, touch and explore.

It should be stressed that not all dyslexics have difficulty with perception and visualisation. Many pupils show strengths in maths and have no such problems – in fact, interpreting diagrams and drawings is easy for them. It is the assessment of the degree of difficulty being experienced in perception and visualisation skills that is difficult to ascertain. Many of our children do indeed possess good powers of visualisation and, combined with their vivid imaginations, have become fine artists. Many of our finest architects are dyslexic.

Poor conceptual understanding

For success in mathematics it is essential that the underlying concepts behind any algorithm, working strategy or formula are understood. This is particularly true for the dyslexic child who may be spending a lot of time doing tedious reinforcing exercises in an attempt to overcome deficits in memory. For example, a child may be able to work out the area of a rectangle but have no concept of what the word 'area' means. He may have fixed in his mind 'Oh, area is when you multiply, perimeter is when you add.' Without a knowledge and understanding of underlying mathematical concepts, a pupil will approach the subject as a composite of discrete bits of unrelated knowledge. Mathematics topics interlink both horizontally and vertically, but without conceptual awareness any interlinking within this web of knowledge and understanding will fail to materialise, and knowledge learnt in one area will not be applied in another. Arithmetic, algebra, geometry and trigonometry and all associated topics contained within their boundaries will remain for the conceptually weak child as discrete unrelated entities.

It is not just dyslexic children who may be weak at conceptual understanding in mathematics; a good proportion of the population would have benefited from a maths education that focused on understanding the subject rather than simply number crunching. When I have lectured at dyslexia conferences and regional staff training days I have asked the gathered audience to quickly give me the answer to the question, 'What is a half divided by a half?' It is a very lonely voice that is heard giving the correct answer; it is being drowned out by over 90 per cent shouting out 'a quarter!' When I rephrase the question and ask, 'How many halves go into a half?' then of course all agree instantly, 'It's one!' Looking at a question from a different angle, drawing a sketch, creating a visual image, handling concrete apparatus or simply putting the numbers into a story can help. One child I taught recently was given the question 3 – 2 + 4, and he gave the answer 16. He had set his work out as follows:

$$\begin{array}{c} 3 - 2 + 4 = \\ 1 \quad\;\; 6 \end{array}$$

He was more than happy with his answer, checking it through repeatedly (3 – 2 = 1, 2 + 4 = 6, Answer 16). Only when we put the numbers into a short story did he understand the question: 'Harry had three cakes and ate two; he then received four more; how many did he have now?' It is important that we understand why our children get questions wrong so that we can correct their errors and rectify any misconceptions, but it is just as important to understand how they get things right. This will give us as teachers an insight into how their minds are working and what state of cognitive development they have reached. For example, three children might solve the question 'what is 25 + 9?' in three different ways, each way displaying a different level of understanding.

Firstly 25 + 9 = 25 counting on 9 on their fingers	Answer 34
Secondly 25 + 9 = 5 + 9 = 14, carry 1, 2 + 1 = 3	Answer 34
Thirdly 25 + 9 = 25 + 10 = 35, take away 1	Answer 34

By being aware of their cognitive level, we can thus design lessons to suit their level of ability.

Dyslexic children need, more than others, to understand the maths they are being taught and have difficulty coping with several alternative approaches, so we should focus on strategies that are simple to conceptualise and comprehend. Take, for example, the circumference of a circle. There is the 'inductive' approach where the formula $C = 2\pi r$ is given. 'Learn it and use it, whether you understand it or not.' (This is the way I was taught.) Then there is the 'deductive' approach, discovering that the diameter always fits around the edge three and a bit times, therefore the circumference = the diameter multiplied by three and a bit, $C = d \times \pi$. Empathising with the dyslexic child, I know which method I would like to be taught. There are many such examples, particularly in the field of 'space and shape', where learning could be facilitated so easily if only we focused primarily on developing concepts. To take another example: the area of a trapezium. Inductively we could be given the formula:

$$\text{Area} = \frac{A + B}{2} \times \text{Ht}. \text{ Learn it and use it.}$$

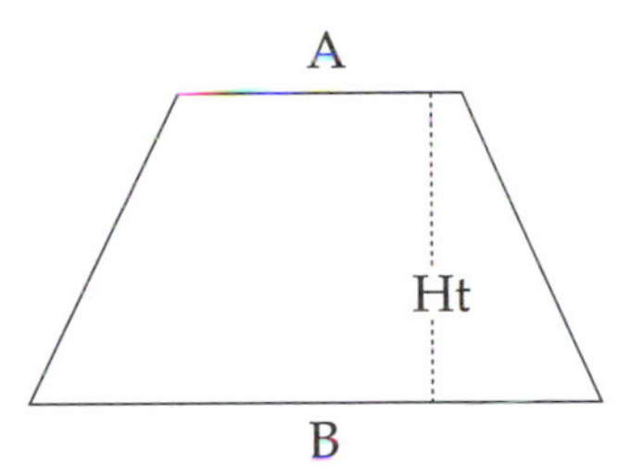

Deductively, on the other hand, the area is the average of the parallel lengths × the width between them. The latter method links directly to the strategy for finding the areas of squares, rectangles and parallelograms and is therefore no great abstract leap forward. By teaching in such a way, we have developed concepts, forged horizontal links to similar topics and moved upwards vertically in our knowledge of the subject.

Before moving on to the next section where I shall be considering children's different learning styles, let us remind ourselves that not all dyslexic children are poor at maths. Occasionally we encounter a spark of genius. Dominic liked to work a lot in his head; the way I had taught him to do long multiplication was far too long-winded, he said, and it meant he had to write too much down, so he developed his own method which he much preferred.

Example

$$\begin{array}{ccccc} & 3 & 1 & 5 & 6 \times \\ & & & 2 & 4 \\ {\scriptstyle 1} & {\scriptstyle 1} & {\scriptstyle 3} & {\scriptstyle 2} & \\ \hline 7 & 5 & 7 & 4 & 4 \end{array}$$

His sequence of working was as follows:

$4 \times 6 = 24$
Carry the 2, write down the 4
$4 \times 5 = 20$ remember
$2 \times 6 = 12$ remember
Add the 12 + 20 + the 2 you have carried = 34
Carry the 3 write down the 4
$4 \times 1 = 4$ remember
$2 \times 5 = 10$ remember
Add the 10 + 4 + the 3 you have carried = 17
Carry the 1 write down the 7
$4 \times 3 = 12$ remember
$2 \times 1 = 2$ remember
Add the 2 + 12 + the 1 you have carried = 15
Carry the 1 write down the 5
$2 \times 3 = 6$
Add on the 1 you have carried = 7
Write down the 7

It works out – with a little practice you might find it quicker.
What sort of mind does Dominic have? Read on.

Mathematical learning profile

The National Numeracy Strategy acknowledges that within any class of children there will exist a variety of learning styles, and the fact that different children will work and problem solve in a number of different ways is to be encouraged. A good classroom teacher will be able to spot the individualistic approaches that are adopted by those in his or her class in an attempt to cope with the subject, and will be able to adapt his or her teaching to suit the needs of the individual pupils. It is a sorry state of affairs when a child who has enjoyed maths and has been doing well in the subject moves up to another class to find a new teacher who has only one teaching style, and that this style may be totally different from and unsympathetic to the child's needs. A mistaken diagnosis may result, and the child may be labelled as having a lack of ability in the subject, when all that is needed is a matching of the teaching to the child's individual learning personality.

The two extremes of learning personalities can be analysed as follows: **Quantitative** at one end of the scale and **qualitative** at the other (Sharma 1989), or **inchworm** versus **grasshopper** (Chinn and Ashcroft 1993). Let us now consider each in turn.

Firstly the **quantitative** learner. He is a person who has an analytical or sequential view of mathematics. They are rule followers and like to follow given procedures. They tackle their maths by looking for specific methods and progress in a step-by-step manner, rather like following a cooking recipe, in their quest for the correct answer.

Secondly the **qualitative** learner. He has a mathematics learning personality that allows him to develop a visualistic overview of a problem. This holistic approach relies a good deal on intuition before a problem is broken down into its component parts and solved, often in a most unconventional way.

Summary

Quantitative learner

- Works methodically step by step.
- Likes to follow rules and formulae.
- Needs to understand why things work.
- Numbers used as given, no diversification.
- Methodical presentation and layout of work.
- Confused by alternative solutions.
- Unlikely to verify their work.

Qualitative learner

- Has an intuitive nature.
- Employs visual imagery, enjoys geometry.
- Can estimate and think ahead.
- Sees relationships between concepts and procedures.
- Explores different routes and strategies.
- Dislikes routine procedures, makes careless mistakes.
- Works in head, reluctant to show working out.

These 'mathematics learning personalities' (Sharma) are displayed again and again outside the maths classroom. I have noticed during many years teaching at East Court that there exists, to a degree, a relationship between an individual's mathematics learning style and his general overall personality. The quantitative child is often an anxious child relying on rules and a structure into which he fits his life, whereas the qualitative child is more carefree, taking risks and generally more laid back. This is reflected in their other subjects and interests. In a science practical lesson one will be methodically recording data in a clear and structured way, producing a precise write-up with clear, neat diagrams and graphs. The other will be excited about experimentation, full of questions 'what if ... ?', wanting to diversify but not keen to put pen to paper.

In the computing lesson, faced with a new program or educational game, one will want to read and understand the instructions first before gingerly advancing onto the next step. The other will dive in head first trying it out with little fear, learning from his mistakes and eventually, through experimentation, succeeding. During model making there are those who religiously follow the instructions, progressing step by step as instructed, and others who gain success after making errors on the way, having simply studied the picture on the front of the box. In a few years time I know how each personality will go about assembling his first purchase of a piece of 'flat packed' furniture.

It is by understanding what makes our children tick both inside and outside the classroom that we can best serve their individual needs and prepare them for their senior schools and adult lives. It is true to say that only a few children are at the extreme ends of the quantitative/qualitative continuum, most are somewhere in between, having characteristics of both styles. In mathematics it is the pupil who is best able to recognise the structure, components and patterns within a question and who is then capable of following recognised set procedures to arrive at the answer, who will ultimately have the most success in this subject. He possesses the ability both to conceptualise and then to apply his knowledge correctly. As teachers it is highly important to recognise the individuality of our pupils, to recognise their strengths and weaknesses and in so doing, become better equipped to develop a teaching strategy that will help them to cope with their learning difficulties. It is also important that this information is shared with other subject staff, documented and passed on to their new schools. The effective teaching of mathematics should therefore focus on a diagnostic analysis of each child's strengths and weaknesses. It needs to be related to an individual's cognitive style and via a flexible teaching outlook and a knowledge of the structure of the subject, a programme of learning can be constructed that will give support and encouragement, thereby fostering a positive attitude towards the subject.

Remember, children may not learn from the way you teach, therefore teach in the way that suits their learning. The rewards of success may be as great for you as they are for the dyslexic child.

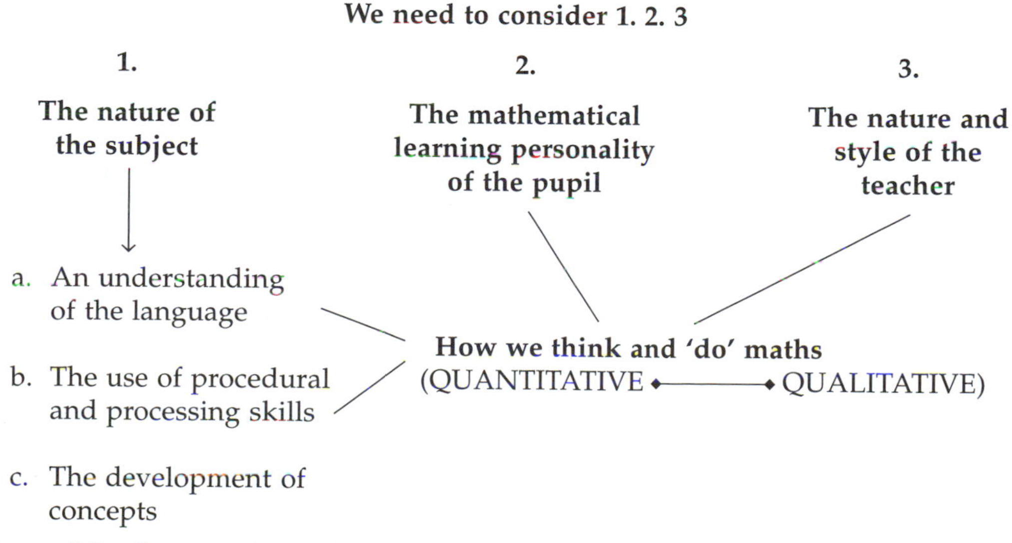

Figure 3.2 Success in mathematics

4 ICT: curriculum, monitoring, activities and support

Tom Broughton

In this chapter Tom Broughton shares the curriculum and monitoring approaches taken with our children in ICT. A brief overview of schemes of work and sample pro-forma for educational planning and assessment are given, as well as a brief description of activities.

ICT (information and communication technology) is, of course, an important part of the National Curriculum but it is also a subject at which many dyslexics can excel. There are some areas where there may be difficulties; obviously word processing is absolutely crucial for dyslexics but may be difficult for some due to expressive writing difficulties. This chapter outlines some elements of an ICT curriculum with examples of procedures.

The following basic principles of an ICT curriculum, as well as some of the teaching discussed later, are relevant for all pupils, whether dyslexic or not.

ICT learning should:

- Enable a pupil to feel at ease with the subject and comfortable with the teacher and with the other pupils in the group.
- Enable each pupil to develop, within his capabilities, the skills and understandings for everyday life; particularly having in mind the impact of 'the information superhighway' and the demands for discernment it implies, quite apart from the system skills required to engage with it.
- Enable each pupil to develop a feel for ICT and thus to produce appropriate, well-presented written work understanding the importance of the intended audience.
- Provide each pupil with such ICT as may be needed for the study of other subjects.
- Help each pupil to develop, as far as is possible, an appreciation and enjoyment of ICT.

Objectives

- To give the opportunity to practise keyboard and presentational skills for the pupils' written work and thus successfully confront and master some of their specific difficulties. They should, therefore, know how to use a desktop publisher (or word processor), a spreadsheet, a database in a graphic user interface and a programming language.
- To consolidate and practise the fundamental skills of operating system control for individual machines.
- To offer problem solving, including the appreciation of ICT in everyday situations.
- To foster the ability to think clearly and to envisage answers to programming problems in a structured manner.
- To promote the development of skills needed to produce and manipulate graphic images.
- To provide appropriate practical work to be conducted in all learning areas.

The above objectives will only be achievable with an understanding of the specific difficulties of the dyslexic child. These will include short-term memory difficulties, poor language and reading ability, problems of personal organisation, sequencing difficulties and directional disorientation, to name but a few. The building of confidence is crucial, as are organisation, including neat recording and filing of work and the importance of availability of equipment, thinking ahead and keyboard skills.

The curriculum and its delivery

We focus on four main attainment targets:

1. desktop publishing (DTP) – word processing (WP)
2. graphics (Painting and Vector types)
3. programming (Logo)
4. handling data (databases and spreadsheets)

(We shall be adding HTML to this list as a basis for the production of web pages that will, initially, be published on the school intranet.)

These targets are broken down into subsets of skills and it is the delivery of these skills that is the focus of the detailed structure of lessons. The general breakdown is rather broad and has been done using 'mind mapping' methods, which are subsequently reformatted as the lists given in Table 4.1; the above attainment targets are addressed by these specific skills.

Medium-term plans and time for delivery

With this skeleton in place it is possible to devise a realistic course of work for each group based on the amount of teaching time available to them, and this is set out in an example in Table 4.2. Generally each group gets one 40-minute session per week in the information and communication technology (ICT) room with an ICT specialist, the exception being the 'leaving' group (12–13 years) who get two such single sessions per week. Double sessions are not recommended, due to our pupils' difficulties in maintaining effective focus for that length of time.

This is probably a minimum level of formal input by the school to ensure that our children achieve the levels of ICT fluency and understanding they will need to carry them through their school careers to at least GCSE. In addition to this ICT input, each group has one English lesson per week in our seven-station IT room, providing further practice of text manipulation or other written language-oriented tasks.

The matter of deciding the course content, the time, teacher and equipment resources for its delivery is crucially important. The DfES/QCA suggested schemes of work for ICT at Key Stages 1, 2 and 3 are very useful guides in this matter. The aims and purposes section for Key Stages 1 and 2 is particularly relevant, though time allocation is left at a distribution of the suggested units over three terms, rather begging the question of levels of detail to be addressed within the individual unit. The Key Stage 3 time recommendations (which affect our older groups) are far more detailed, but represent a formidable demand on resources, leaving very little time for system maintenance and administration.

It should be noted that keyboarding skills are taught separately, each group getting one session per week. This is based on a ten-stage 'typing programme'. The first five stages are linked to one, then two, then three fingers etc., starting at the 'home key'. A certificate is given for each stage achieved (touch typing, no looking). Once Stage 4 or 5 has been reached, children are encouraged to get their own laptop. This can then be used in any classroom as the school is networked. The laptop can be plugged in to the Local Area Network (LAN) for classwork, homework, editing and tutorial work with a teacher, or to download information programs.

Stages 6 to 10 of our typing are linked to written language; essentially speed and copy practice for key words, two and three-syllable words, particular letter patterns and so on. Pupils bring their improving keyboard skills to IT lessons but keyboard 'correctness' (while praiseworthy) is not allowed to stand between pupils and their use and understanding of IT skills.

Table 4.1 ICT subskills

Introducing Information Technology

Recognising Types of Computers
Working with the CPU
Working with Input and Output Devices
Working with Memory Storage Devices
Defining Types of Computer Memory
Defining Types of Software
Using Operating System Software and Application Software

Using Electronic Mail and the Internet

Using Computers in the Home, at Work and in School
Viewing a Changing World
Using Computers Properly and Safely
Working with Security and Preventing Computer Viruses

Internet Basics

Carrying out WWW searches
Working with Web Pages
Using Email Basics
Sending Email Messages
Using the Computer
Working with Computers

Using Startup and Shutdown

Reviewing the Desktop
Using Menus and Dialogue Boxes
Using the Operating System
Using Files/Folders/Shortcuts
Using Printers

Desktop Publishing Part 1

Working with DTPs
Working with the Embedded Help Systems
Using Basic Document Skills
Checking Spelling
Using Basic Text Editing
Using Character Formatting
Using Paragraph Formatting
Using Document Formatting
Setting Tabs and Indenting Paragraphs
Using Numbers and Bullets
Working with Headers and Footers

Data Handling

Understanding Data and Information
Exploring Spreadsheets
Using Basic Spreadsheet Skills
Working with Ranges
Creating Simple Formulas
Copying and Moving Data
Printing Spreadsheets
Using Setup Facilities for Printing
Formatting Numbers and Text
Working with Columns and Rows
Formatting Cells
Using Large Spreadsheets
Managing Spreadsheets
Working with HTML Files
Using Paste Special
Creating Charts
Managing Data and Files

Desktop Publishing Part 2

Inserting Dates and Symbols
Working with Tables
Applying Borders and Shading
Working with Columns
Using Find and Replace
Working with Hyphenation
Using Mail Merge
Importing Data Files
Inserting Graphic Files
Using Graphing Facilities

Drawing Part 1 and Part 2

Bitmap Graphics
Identifying the Tools and Their Uses
Using Brush and Pencil to Edit
Choosing the Right Tool
Working Pixel by Pixel and Using Masks
Building a Library of Reuseable Images
Using Clip Art Libraries
Vector Graphics
Understanding the 'Vector' Metaphor
Drawing Objects and Lines
Editing Objects and Lines
Colour Filling, Blending and Interpolating
Working with Layers

Table 4.2 Example of educational plan for teaching group (age 12–13 years) set 7 (Time per week 80 minutes)

Autumn	Spring	Summer
Word Processing and DTP + Graphics	*Logo + Graphics*	*Data Handling: Database + Spreadsheet*
DTP Understand that different readers have different needs in addressing written work. Accurate keyboarding (with 600 words max. of 12 pt. text) to enter, save, edit and print out that text. Proof-read and amend text. Be able to 'stripe' and 'block' select so as to separate header, banner and body text and format, selecting fonts and point sizes appropriately, resizing and positioning of text and graphic objects. Create numbered column layouts.	LOGO Gain familiarity, through use, with simple commands. Understand what a computer program is. Use the editor to produce programs to draw geometric shapes (maths, input). Incorporate variables in these programs and know the difference between a variable and its value. Understand recursion. Use conditional statements to control looping programs. Produce an animated cartoon or 'branching' game.	DATABASE Make use of learnt skills to produce final year science project. (a) Use conditional searches to 'home in' on the required details using a wide variety of sources including the Internet, books and CD-ROMs. (b) Download that information to a DTP. (c) Collect information and enter, save, load, edit and print out that information into a self-prepared database form from a properly constructed data capture form.
GRAPHICS Use of 'Vector graphic' application to independently produce graphic related to text and merge into that text. Use editing facilities to produce all required elements of a graphic from basic shapes, understanding the masking effects of layers. Increase rate of working by knowing and using keyboard short cuts.	GRAPHICS Use of 'Vector graphic' application to independently produce a display piece using all skills learnt. Show understanding of the printing effects of choosing different levels of ink saturation. Save, load, edit and print out.	SPREADSHEET Collect numerical (science or own interest input) and enter it into a spreadsheet. Thence edit, save, load, print out. Perform arithmetic on rows and columns to find sums, products, differences and averages. Be able to format entries into a spreadsheet. Save in Vector graphics format for inclusion in text or graphics file.

Email and Internet

No time provision is made for the development of skills needed to use email or Internet within these plans. In the context of our small, independent specialist school, email is a main communication route between our pupils and their parents, siblings and friends at home and at other schools. There is, therefore, considerable enthusiasm for the activity and the skills are 'shown' rather than taught in the informal context of evening free time. This is made particularly easy by the web-based email facilities provided on the school LAN to which all pupils have access using their own user name and password. The network home page has a direct link to the email system and is available at initial log on. Having accessed the email area, pupils go through a second level of security with the same user name and password and their home address is written into their personal address book as part of the year start administration tasks. Any other addresses they add to their own address book as required.

Pupil access to the World Wide Web is achieved through the same home page, which offers the usual facilities to enter known Web addresses and has permanent links to the BBC home page and the better-known search engines (Yahoo UK, Google, Dogpile, AltaVista, Yahooligans).

Clearly all incoming and outgoing communications are put through a 'censorship' filter, which checks text and web sites against a list of keywords. Our Internet service provider ensures that sites that offer purchasing facilities are only accessible to teachers and we allow chat room access to no one. Parents and children are informed of this.

Detailed plans, records and assessments

As ICT (with the exception of Logo) is largely a training rather than an educative exercise, it is sensible to have tick sheets that enable teacher and pupil to know what the required skills are and when they have been encountered and mastered. The five tick boxes (I write dates in them) show developing mastery; A being first encounter with, and E independent mastery of, an activity. As each area of the curriculum is introduced, so each pupil gets an A4 record sheet (in a plastic wallet) to put into his ICT folder. This also forms the basis of the initial discussion with the group when we talk about the aims we have for whatever job it is that we are going to use to provide a context for the skills we are working on. We do not try to tick off every skill on a sheet before moving on to another, indeed achieving a tick in a new context is one of the (unspoken) aims of the system. That said, we try never to have more than three sheets open at any one time and this we normally achieve. This system works particularly well with monitoring and recording the achievement of targets for email and Internet skills which are delivered informally. Pupils quickly get to know what the expectations are to get a tick and so seek to demonstrate work they think of as worthy. The achievement of the intermediate and the final levels are linked to the school reward system. Perhaps surprisingly, this link to rewards also motivates the (otherwise worldly) 12 and 13 year-olds. This gives useful structure to our children's learning and allows both the less practised and the able to proceed to the point where they need support, at their own rate. Generally they will, without prompting, print out work to support particular attainments and bring it forward for assessment.

An example of a record tick sheet is given in Table 4.3. Note it is usually an A4 page. There is a Basic, an Intermediate and an Advanced sheet for each pupil. (I am happy to share my other record and assessment sheets with interested readers – four attainment targets and three levels each.)

Pupil activities

Choosing activities in which to set this work is the subject of a large body of published work to which I am reluctant to add. Certainly the old maxim 'start where the children are' is a valuable guide, but it is useful if you can start from where you are as well. The activities we present to our pupils are always improved if we can bring our own interests and (above all) enthusiasms to them. The genuinely stuck should refer to the DfES teacher guides for initial safe guidance that will ensure that all the curriculum is covered, for there is no difference between the scope of work offered to our children and that offered in any other school.

So I offer, with notes as to purpose, work done by our pupils. Sometimes this has arisen from my direct instruction, 'Copy this; you are allowed a maximum of three typos'; sometimes from their pursuit of a piece of work from another subject, 'Please sir, can we use a spreadsheet to compare the running costs of ten household electrical appliances?'

Table 4.3 Example of record and assessment skills

Name **Date……………………..**	**Word Processing Intermediate**	**A**	**B**	**C**	**D**	**E**
Plan document and enter text	Plan a document that fills two or more pages of text. It should include page numbers, a header or footer, a footnote and bullet points. Enter text.					
Number pages	Set up automatic page numbering.					
Create a header or footer	Create either a header or footer for the document so that it appears on every page.					
Change margins	Change the left and right margins. Change the top and bottom margins.					
Create columns	Format some or all of your text so that it is in two newspaper-style columns.					
Use macros	Create a macro that types out your name and use it in the document.					
Create footnote	Create a footnote.					
Create section headings and bullet points	Create two or more section headings. Use two or more bullet points.					
Create a table of contents and a title page	Create a title page. Create a table of contents using dot leaders. Make sure date numbering is suppressed on the first of these two pages.					
Preview and print specific pages	Preview your document. Print the table of contents only. Check that it is correct and make any necessary standard changes. Print the rest of the document.					

Examples of pupil activities

1. WP/DTP

Initial exercises should be short, preferably amusing and, if possible, of sufficient merit to bear scrutiny:

> The sausage is a cunning bird,
> with features long and wavy;
> It swims about the frying pan,
> and makes its nest in gravy.

Such a passage is entered in 28 point sans serif onto a ready headed-up page, proof-read by looking at the error highlighting and listening to the speak-back facilities of the DTP. When correct, it is saved and printed out.

It is then reloaded, edited (usually by changing the margins and/or the point size), resaved and printed out.

The printout and the on-screen file is then used for the basis of discussion – what if:

- we centre justified?
- we fully justified?
- we put the text at the top/bottom/side of the page?
- we used a different font for each line?
- we used different colours for the text?

I choose questions that will get the children to explore the areas appropriate to the curriculum but the technique can lead to interesting new ideas and this level of discussion is never wasted time. Obviously, 'what if we illustrated it?' comes up and that leads easily into graphics work.

As time goes on classes are called on to take over the production of the news-sheet and practise entering quite big (600-word) text files. They are then expected to format those files for different readerships (senior pupils write stories for the younger groups), attach the files to emails, and carry out a full range of text and document manipulations. I liaise with the English and typing teacher on levels and pupils also undertake WP work in story writing and other English work. As mentioned earlier, once children reach Level 4/5 (out of 10) on our typing program, they are encouraged to obtain a laptop or equivalent with keyboard memory with a LAN connection for the school network. Any work, whether in class or homework, can then be done on a laptop.

2. Graphics

The purpose of the graphics content has little to do with addressing the artistic education of children (although a large number do seem to benefit in this area). It is a means to a number of ends – understanding the functions of the tools, having the confidence to select them, starting and having the persistence to finish a piece of work, editing, saving, loading and printing. Improving the fluency of mouse handling is an important objective to us, as a number of our children have dyspraxic problems. These general, underlying skills once mastered lead on to other areas – does the image do what was intended, illustrate the text, help with the assembly of the radio-controlled car or demonstrate the mathematical point? Finally, the completed files can be used to provide practice in the use of a number of different files in a single DTP document. All the work that children do is saved, either to their network area or (more commonly in the case of graphics) on their own floppy discs. This enables them to build up their own clip art libraries. Children with serious confidence problems start their graphics 'career' with clip art, which they can then edit to create their own images. This situation does not arise often and, when it does, does not last long.

Figure 4.1 The seagull and its deconstruction

Activities include illustrating a piece of word processing work, making a classroom plan which is useful for copying and repositioning objects, page decorations or patterns. Figure 4.1 illustrates how objects can be deconstructed.

3. Logo

Logo is a programming language and it is true that for most pupils programming as 'job training' is nonsense. However, if you are able to interest pupils in programming, studying it in some depth can be valuable for the same reasons that other people benefit from acting, music or being a news reporter: it is a kind of intellectual apprenticeship. What is being learnt is the discipline of serious thinking and of taking pride in work. Its abstraction calls for precise specification and discussion which our children engage in to achieve their self-set aims. The value of this access to the elegant complexities of language that most of our children are ready for cannot be overstated, for it is available without the barriers of spelling and reading that so frustrate them in 'normal' language. Its very difficulties are its strengths; that things go wrong is a blessing. A set of instructions sent to a turtle often results in something unexpected. These 'bugs' are part of the learning process. They do not stop the activity; they are simply a step on the way to further discoveries and deeper understanding.

Most of our Logo work is done in pairs so as to provide a context for relevant discussion of the set work. The note that follows assumes a basic familiarity with Turtle graphics and its commands. The project shown represents all the features of Logo that make the language so valuable in the learning process, and represents work done by pupils in their penultimate year. Command abbreviation means low spelling loads; feedback on the accuracy of the commands is a press of the return key away. Accuracy (or otherwise) is self-mediated, so pupils can choose the point at which they seek support. The fact that the same command sets that drive the turtle on the normal screen are valid within the editor for programming is a great advantage and the Face project (shown in Table 4.4) shows that. The lists of commands (15 for group One (8-year-old) and 97 for the leaving group) represents the achievement of most pupils at that level. Most do better, but a few do need continuous support for their recall of the commands. (Large format wall charts usually provide that support.)

It would be possible to suggest a wide range of activities but there seems little point in restating work widely available elsewhere. In general, the best work is done by children following their own enthusiasms and interests, fostered and facilitated by a teacher who knows them and has a comfortable knowledge of the potential of the program. (This, of course, is the central truth about all teaching of ICT or anything else.)

This command list (Table 4.4) will produce a face as a 'Turtle drawing'. It can be printed out to make a hard copy and represents the average expectation for our 10–11 year-olds working outside the editor. It is also a common first attempt to program such a face in the editor. This is known as a 'string' program. The annotation list (left-hand column) is the first step in imposing structure on this program and leads to the expanded list.

Imposing the structure can now begin. The method is to write the program as a logical set of small subprocedures – in this case start, outline, startel, eye1, etc.

4. Data handling

Data handling is covered as two different working areas, spreadsheets and databases. Spreadsheets will initially give the context of the maths curriculum, as they are used to address the ideas of central tendency (mean, mode, median) and spread (range, deviation) of groups of numbers. Thus we can work in single 'columns' or 'rows', identify cells and use column headings to introduce the ideas of data as coded information. This initial work is done with prepared sheets which are downloaded from the school LAN and it is not until pupils are familiar with the appearance and understand the use of a spreadsheet that we move on to the creation of their own column and row headings and subsequent data entry. This initial sheet is produced over a set of these lessons. The first one invites

Table 4.4 Example of logo program: face

The method is to write the program as a SUPERPROCEDURE called Face with a logical set of small subprocedures within it thus:

TO FACE
Start outline
Startel eye1
Starte2 eye2
Startr2 ear2
Startr1 ear1
Startno nose
Startmo mouth
END

However, each of the above, e.g. eye1, has its own commands. The detailed command list is as follows:

LOGO	A PROGRAM FOR A FACE	
	Program Start	TO FACE
		pu It 90 fd 300
	sets the start position	rt 90 bk 300 pd
		fd 600 rt 90
		fd 600 rt 90
		fd 600 rt 90
	draws the face outline	fd 600 rt 90
		fd 500 rt 90
	sets the start position for eye1	pu fd 100 rt 90
		pd fd 150 It 90
		fd 150 It 90
		fd 150 It 90
	draws eye1	fd 150 It 90
	sets the start position for eye2	It 90 pu fd 250 pd
	draws eye2	repeat 4 (fd 150 rt 90)
		fd 150 rt 90
		fd 150 It 90
	sets the start position for ear2	pu fd 100
		pd fd 125 It 90
		fd 125 It 90
	draws ear2 and moves to ear1	fd 125 pu fd 600
		pd fd 125 It 90
		fd 125 It 90
	draws ear1 and moves to nose	fd 125 pu fd 300
		rt 90 fd 100
	draws nose	pd repeat 4 (fd 50 It 90)
	sets the start position for mouth	pu fd 150 rt 90
	draws mouth	pd fd 200 It 90
		fd 50 It 90
		fd 400 It 90
		fd 50 It 90
		fd 200
	Program end	END

the class to set up a 'business plan' for a whelk stall (given our seaside location!). Firstly, we decide what we are going to sell and this produces a range of suggestions from chips and cans of Coke to lobster bisque. These suggestions are refined down to ten selling lines which become column 1.

We then discuss the information we need to enter in order to control costs and know profits (never forgetting the hire of the barrow). By the end of this first lesson, we will

Table 4.5 'My Whelk Stall' spreadsheet

	A	B	C	D	E	F	G	H
4	My Whelk Stall							
5								
6	Product	Buy P	o/head	Profit	Tax	Sell P	No Sold	Tot/Prof
7	Whelks	10.0	5.0	30.0	6.0	51.0	70.0	
8	Coke	25.0	10.0	75.0	15.0	115.0	100.0	
9	Burgers	50.0	20.0	150.0	30.0	230.0	30.0	
10	Cockles	30.0	12.0	90.0	18.0	138.0	70.0	
11	Crisps	12.0	5.0	36.0	2.0	55.0	140.0	
12	Prawns	60.0	22.0	180.0	16.0	278.0	70.0	
13	Mussels	30.0	12.0	90.0	150.0	282.0	70.0	
14	Chips	70.0	25.0	210.0	10.0	315.0	90.0	
15	Ice Cream	20.0	8.0	60.0	4.0	92.0	140.0	
16								
17	Total							

have committed the sheet to the board and everybody is usually satisfied with it. The second session is a recap of the previous work and then the business of data entry, checking and printing out. This takes patience and the acceptance of initial error. These errors (and they will occur) are very useful, for they form the basis of further learning of the skills of editing. Table 4.5 demonstrates a range of formatting skills for spreadsheet layout, although the numbers entered are rather random. The only relationship is that the profit should be three times the cost price. The third lesson 'tidies up' the numbers and, if appropriate, allows the discussion of the idea of percentages and the various column and row addition procedures.

Databases are initially approached via the study of a prepared database. 'Kings and Queens of England' is popular, as are census returns for individual towns. Time is allowed for the free perusal of all records and this allows for the ideas of 'field' and 'record' to be explored and the ideas of sorting and searching to be introduced. By the end of the second lesson, simple searches, for example 'How many kings called Edward have we had?' and sorts, e.g. 'The kings and queens are listed in chronological order, now sort them into the order of length of reign, starting with the longest' are carried out, saved and printed. The third lesson is devoted to further searches and the incorporation of the results of these searches into desktop publishing applications. Once basic skills are mastered by most of the group, the class will propose Internet searches; detailed results over a number of seasons for favourite football clubs; names of characters in Gilbert and Sullivan operas; sharks, poisonous spiders – these are all grist to the information mill. By the time the curriculum spiral has turned and they are in their second year, collecting and organising enough information to support work in other curriculum areas (particularly science, geography and humanities) has become the norm for this work.

5 Accessing the curriculum: procedures and study skills

Anne Bailey

Helping dyslexics is also about delivering the curriculum to them in a way that they can access. Following a general introduction by myself, Anne Bailey gives practical examples of using videos, appropriate worksheets and cloze procedures in humanities and science.

Introduction

This chapter looks at how the dyslexic individual can access the curriculum. By this we mean whether the individual can still learn in subjects outside of English and mathematics, where he may be having specialised help. We will be looking at some general principles, as well as providing details of study skills that may be helpful in these areas.

A key component of teaching dyslexic children is modifying the curriculum. This is sometimes called 'differentiation' or 'modified mainstream curriculum' or similar terminology. The important point here is to recognise that you are trying to allow children to learn a subject area without too much dependence on written language. This implies that one is not set a chapter in a science book to read, followed by an essay or comprehension on the topic. It is likely that the level of reading would be too difficult for the dyslexic child, despite the fact that his understanding of the material would be good. This parallels the discrepancy between comprehension skills and decoding skills in English.

It is important to remember not to expect a dyslexic child to rely on notes or information given by dictation or to be copied from the blackboard. At a recent INSET day two of our ex-pupils, both at university, gave a talk on what it was like to be dyslexic. They said that one of the most important things a subject teacher could do was provide copies of notes/ information etc. in the form of appropriate handouts. They could then focus on the lesson and not worry about catching up on note taking which was a nightmare for them. Some older dyslexics tape their lectures and then go back to make notes from them at a later date. One of the students also commented on the irony of having had his acceptance to university on the same day as a report telling him he had a spelling age of 12 years.

In many areas such as humanities or science, teachers will teach by discussing the topic and requiring the student to take his own notes or from dictation. Trying to summarise from someone speaking is a difficult enough task for anyone, let alone a dyslexic, and therefore should be avoided. Similarly, the teacher who tries to dictate in the closing moments of the lesson all of the material covered will end up with one or two words or lines from the dyslexic pupil – if they are lucky.

The above of course relates to the difficulties in auditory working memory that dyslexics have, but the other alternative is copying from a board. Again, teachers often cover the board with their notes and ask pupils to copy them down. Often there may be further notes to put on the blackboard, and when the teacher asks, 'Have you finished this? Okay, I'll wipe it off', the poor dyslexic student may still be struggling to finish the first line. With visual memory and motor control difficulties, copying from the board is a really difficult task for dyslexics and should be kept to a minimum or avoided altogether.

Therefore a basic start in modifying the curriculum for dyslexics would be to provide appropriate notes and worksheets for them (examples are given later in the chapter). Ideally, appropriate worksheets for humanities and science such as cloze procedures or frameworks are absolutely crucial if one is unable to get so-called 'High-Low' material. Many publishers now have high-interest low-reading age materials which are ideal for dyslexic children, but there are not so many available for subject areas such as science, geography, history and so on. In general, the expectations should be high for content and knowledge of subject materials, but low for written language, be it reading text, copying from a board, taking dictation, writing essays or comprehension questions on the subject.

At secondary school level, it is important for the dyslexic individual to take appropriate subjects. These include things like craft, design and technology, ICT, science and so on (although we have just heard that one of our past pupils has been offered a place at Oxford to read history, so this does not apply to all students). Before we look at some very specific study skills and examples of working practice, some general principles are important. The first is to do what would be done in English and maths; that is, to plan lessons carefully, so that there are very small sequential steps. For maximum learning potential in dyslexic children, the material to be learnt needs to be very well structured and accumulated gradually.

In general terms, it is better to work from the concrete to the abstract, to check constantly and monitor what the pupil is doing. It is necessary to work from one area at a time, to make sure that the link between the different areas and subject components is understood and new experiences are linked to past ones.

It is crucial not to give homework in the rushed last few minutes of the lesson. Make sure that the child does understand exactly what is required and that the material that he takes away with him for his homework is within his reading and spelling capacity. For the older students, material that needs to be learnt for examinations should be given to them in note form which is readily understandable. It is also important to know your children well – do not assume that because a child is nodding sagely, he understands what you are talking about. The child may think, 'Unless I nod, I may be picked on'.

A key difficulty for dyslexics is organisation. This implies help for the pupil but also that the teacher should be highly organised.

It is also important to recognise that long pages of text are not necessarily the best way for dyslexics to learn. They may prefer their information on small cards or posters with pictures; it is important to cater to a particular individual's learning style. Keywords are also very useful.

Three major problems when teaching dyslexics are:

1. How to convey information to the pupils.
2. How to ensure that they record it in an accessible medium.
3. How to assess how much information they have retained.

The remainder of this chapter will offer ideas on how to manage these problems. It will be noted that a key feature is reinforcing the learning approach undertaken in the specialist English class.

Managing the Curriculum

Videos

Most children are comfortable with videos. They regard them as a treat and many dyslexics visibly relax when they realise they are not being asked to read a book. While bearing in mind that overkill must be avoided, the multiplicity of educational videos currently available means that there is a wide range of high quality and easily accessible information to be used.

Training pupils to get the best from videos means that varying approaches must be used, to ensure that all students receive the full benefit of them. Many dyslexics will have great difficulty in making notes or answering questions *while the video is running*. They are also likely to be confused if the video is interrupted to enable notes to be taken. It is a good idea to allow the video to be viewed in its entirety as an initial exercise.

The video can then be discussed by all pupils, who contribute the points they remember. At this stage it is best if the teacher records the comments made by pupils. It is incumbent upon the teacher already to have decided on the format of the notes and whether or not the pupils will be required to write or copy any of them. With younger pupils, those with additional difficulties or those with short concentration spans or short-term memory problems, this may take a full lesson.

To reinforce any points that the teacher considers necessary, pupils who have difficulties are often more comfortable with cartoons or sketches that show extracts from the video and to which they can add captions. The teacher may choose to write a series of captions and ask the pupils to illustrate them. Captions may be agreed by a group as a whole with illustrations being a matter for each pupil individually. Illustrations and captions could be provided by the teacher for pupils to match, or teachers could mix these and allocate different tasks to different pupils for the purposes of differentiation. In the example given in Figure 5.1, children were asked to produce a sketch and caption after watching a video about competition. They illustrated various points on the positive and negative aspects of competition. (Incidently, note the frequent, use of 'competion' for 'competition'.)

Many dyslexic pupils have to be given a great deal of encouragement before they are confident enough to attempt any writing task; these pupils may often respond if work has been pencilled in for them to overwrite. This also serves to encourage correct letter formation and presentation, and enables slower writers to complete work in line with the speed of more able colleagues. As confidence and writing skills improve in individuals, the amount pencilled in may be reduced, allowing the pupil to see that he is making progress.

As pupils become more used to using videos in this way, their concentration while watching a video will increase, their ability to remember what they have seen will also increase, as will their ability to make notes in the format their teacher requires. *It is essential that this format is clearly established at the outset and that changes made to it are made gradually and with full explanation.*

Pupils who use videos regularly will become skilled in these 'debriefing' and note-making sessions, and will soon wish to participate more fully and to demand more complex information. At this point, multi-tasking may be introduced. Classes may be divided into groups and given specific areas of the video to remember. They should be allowed to make rough notes while the video is running *if they choose to do so*. Groups might be arranged to include one good/fast writer who is then given the task of scribe and the groups discuss together the recording of their specific notes. The teacher then acts as collator of the information. The teacher will have, of course, already analysed the video, extracted the required information and prepared the necessary notes which can be handed to the groups to ensure that each group has a whole set of notes.

The preparation of notes is also something that can be adapted to suit individual pupils, or groups of pupils. It is sometimes helpful for pupils to be given notes written by hand in a style that is consistent with the style pupils are being encouraged to learn. Fancy fonts or elegant calligraphy may confuse pupils with reading difficulties. It is important for pupils to be comfortable with handwritten *and* printed information.

The way in which these notes can be recorded by pupils is a matter for teachers to decide, in accordance with the requirements of their schemes of work and in line with the abilities of their pupils.

The key to using video tasks is to know your pupils and to ask them to do things that stretch them but do not overwhelm them.

Spider diagrams

Spider diagrams are a simplified form of the 'mind mapping' technique and are an easy way to make notes from any source of information. The main subject is placed at the centre of the web and the relevant points are placed at the end of radiating spokes. It is then possible to draw linking lines to points where connecting features are observed and the resulting diagram should bear some resemblance to a spider's web. More able pupils are able to use the spider diagram to make linear notes or to answer comprehension-style

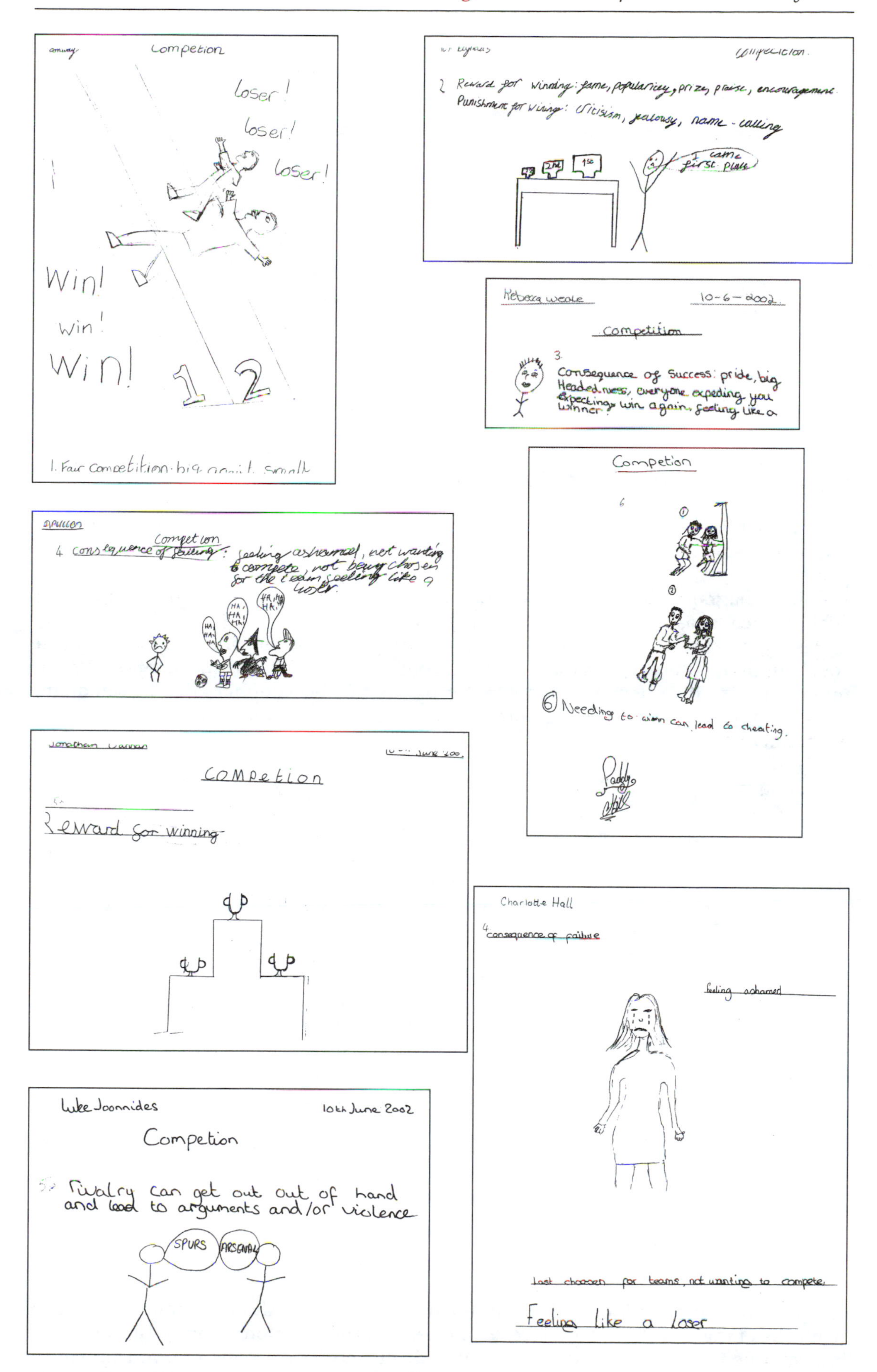

Figure 5.1 An example of a caption exercise produced after watching a video

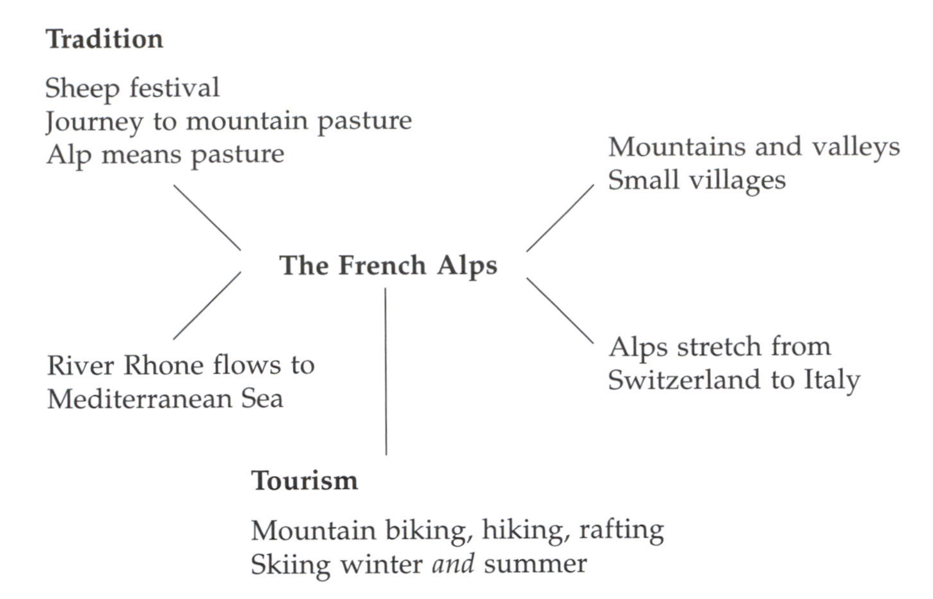

Figure 5.2 Example of spider diagram about the French Alps

questions which may then be assessed in accordance with National Curriculum levels. The spider diagrams may also be used as exam revision aids and even as essay plans.

Spider diagrams can also be used to take notes for class or, better still, be given by subject teachers as a summary of their lessons.

It is my experience that these methods of delivering and recording information encourage concentration, observation, group working, cooperation and individual confidence. The minimum of writing demanded enables the dyslexic to feel confident that he can do the work required. It is a long time before he realises that he is writing whole sentences and eventually paragraphs.

Colouring-in

Sometimes inspectors or other visitors comment that 'they are just colouring'. While we agree that on its own this is not enough, it does have real benefits for dyslexics, who often have very poor pen control. Colouring-in encourages them to practise skills of accuracy, about which they complain when it is called writing or calligraphy. Maps are excellent practice for hand-eye coordination skills and, if instructions are kept to a minimum until good habits become ingrained and each new demand is made with a clear set of simple instructions, pupils will gain confidence in their own abilities. From instructions such as 'colour the coastline in blue', more complex tasks can be set involving the transfer of information from atlases, or from one map to another. Maps can be used in subjects such as history and RE as well as geography, and consistency across the curriculum must be sustained. If, in geography lessons, coastlines are marked with a single blue line, so any map completed for history or RE must have its coastline marked with a single blue line.

The example given in Figure 5.3 will require the child to obtain material to verify the historical accuracy of the costume. He can then go on to plan his own costume for a special event such as the Viking Day we had at school (which consisted of a visit by 'Vikings' with historical stories, games and warfare).

Story telling

Children who have difficulty in reading still love stories. Allowing children to relax while listening is often conducive to increased concentration. Stories can again be brainstormed using spider diagrams, turned into notes, cartoons or even timelines. Cliffhanger endings or gory titbits are excellent for getting pupils to look forward to their next lesson.

Instructions for completion

Using the posters around the classroom, the photographs and the books on the shelves, colour this Viking.

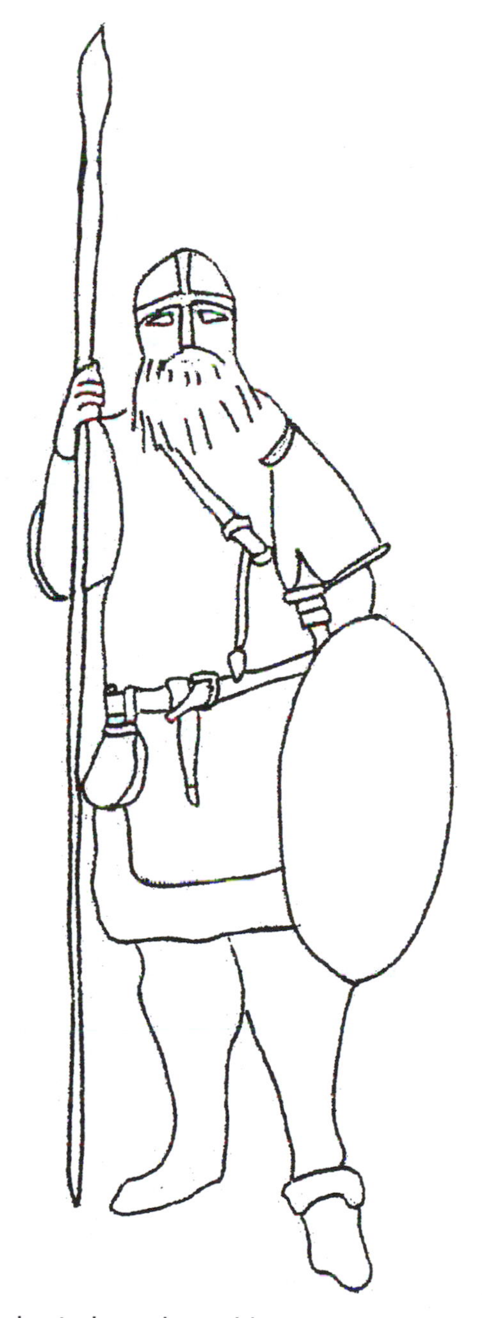

Figure 5.3 A Viking warrior to be coloured in

Any story can be developed into a worksheet specifically designed for use with your individual pupils, thus allowing for differentiation.

Information sheets

A printed sheet with the information you wish your pupils to use is useful. Some dyslexic children are more comfortable with a handwritten sheet if they are more used to your handwriting or if they find printed sheets 'too much like books'. An example is given in figure 5.4. Note that this would be for children whose reading had come on well. Simpler, easier to read ones would be used for weaker readers.

Name .... Date ....

SAMUEL PEPYS

Samuel Pepys lived in London. During the reign of Charles II he worked as a clerk for the Navy. For nine years he kept a diary which gives us a lot of information about life in London. He tells us that London was an overcrowded, noisy and dirty city. The River Thames supplied drinking water but was also the city's sewer. Houses were close together and mostly built of wood.

On 7 June 1665 Samuel wrote 'I did in Drury Lane see two or three houses marked with a red cross upon the doors, and "Lord have mercy upon us" writ there; which was a sad sight for me.'

The plague was back in London!

A 9 o'clock curfew was imposed. The dead were collected in carts and, once the churchyards were full, were buried in large pits. Once a house was identified as having the plague it was shut up with the residents inside whether they were sick or not.

Death lists were printed – 70,000 died altogether.

Questions

1. For whom did Pepys work?
2. How could you describe Pepys' London?
3. How was the River Thames used?
4. What were the houses built of?
5. What was marked on houses with the plague?
6. Where were the dead buried?
7. How many people died altogether?

Figure 5.4 Example of information/comprehension sheet

The details below are for using information sheets in class but they also act as notes for a lesson. The information sheet would be read out with the pupils.

The pupils *must* follow as you read and underline or highlight important points on your instructions. You will have to be prepared to repeat yourself several times. You will also observe your able pupils assisting your less able – do not stop this – the support is confidence building for all concerned. Of course, a learning support assistant is also invaluable here to help maintain focus. Once all the required information has been highlighted or underlined, go through the sheet again pointing out that the underlined or highlighted information corresponds with answers to questions that you wish to be answered and allow the pupils to number the answers. *They must then make an attempt to write the answers in a neat, well-presented form.* If you have ensured a high level of comprehension during the oral session of your lesson, you have given your dyslexic pupils the means to provide themselves with a written record of their ability.

Differentiation can be added by asking a question you have not underlined or highlighted, or by asking them to set an additional question(s) to each other. As pupils become better readers, the underlining and highlighting can be used for *keywords only.* This again becomes a revision technique they can use throughout their educational career.

Some pupils might find it easier to have the 'gap information' printed at the bottom of the sheet or to have a fully completed sheet for reference. As pupils become more skilled readers and writers they are able to use cloze procedures in combination with information from books and videos. Again the sheets can be used for revision purposes.

Cloze exercises are well known to prepare English skills by encouraging the use of context. Here they are used to encourage these skills in other subjects and to provide notes, or even as experiments in science. Two examples are given in Figures 5.5 and 5.6. Pupils copy information into the gaps in pencil, and then ink it over when they are sure they are correct. The inking over also allows for spelling to be checked and presentation

Read through and fill in the missing gaps with the words below.

BUNSEN BURNER OPERATING INSTRUCTIONS

To light a Bunsen burner the air hole is c .... and the gas tap is h .... o .... If you leave the Bunsen burner alight on your bench you want the flame to be clearly seen, so you use a y .... flame, with the air hole c .... To heat with a Bunsen burner use a b .... flame and have the air hole h .... o .... and the gas tap f .... o .... For very strong heating we use a r .... f .... The air hole is fully o .... and the gas tap f .... o ....

Missing words

fully open	flame	blue	closed
yellow	fully on	open	fully on
half open	roaring	half open	

Figure 5.5 Example of science cloze procedure

EXTREME WEATHER – HOT

Greenwich is one of the .... places in England.

Temperatures as high as .... have been recorded.

The warmest places in England are away from .... where layers of cloud act as a .... which stops heat ....

The Prime Meridian of .... passes through Greenwich.

The hottest place in .... is 5,500 miles west of Greenwich.

It is .... in Nevada, USA.

The floor of the valley is .... below sea level.

Temperatures are approximately .... Even at night, with little cloud to ...., temperatures remain at ....

The area is a .... There is no farming and little wildlife.

The landscape of the valley was formed by ....

During winter storms water washes through Death Valley, often in the form of .... This water brings ....

The wind in Death Valley is also hot so .... in buildings and cars is essential.

Figure 5.6 Geography worksheet. Missing words can be provided or be extracted from notes given.

to be improved. Generally, the information to be added is copied from the board. Teachers must ensure that the information is mapped onto the board in the same way as it is to be fitted onto the sheet – this assists pupils who find copying from the board difficult and those who have difficulty in keeping their place.

Exams

It is difficult to assess the abilities of dyslexic pupils if all examinations are written as, obviously, their reading and writing difficulties intrude on the subject matter. Conversely, if all exams are given orally, it is similarly difficult to provide a written assessment. One method that has proved useful is the *tick* or *circle the correct answer* method. This works particularly well when you wish to measure the amount of information pupils have retained. By combining this method with multiple choice answers it is also possible to

Name .... Date ....

HISTORY EXAMINATION GROUP IV JANUARY 2001

1. Draw a line to join the families who fought the Wars of the Roses to their correct symbol. 2 marks

LANCASTER	**JONES**	**SMITH**	**YORK**
YELLOW ROSE	**RED ROSE**	**WHITE ROSE**	**BLUE ROSE**

2. Richard III was killed at which battle? Circle the correct answer. 1 mark

BORISTOWN **BLUE CITY** **BOSWORTH**

3. If Tudor society is a pyramid, draw an arrow to show where you would put the king. 2 marks

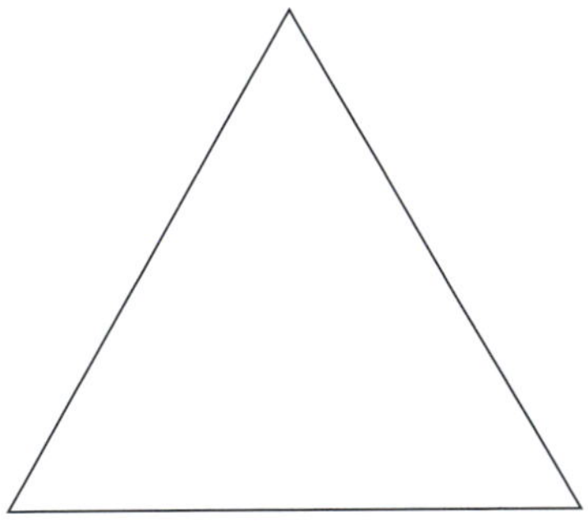

4. Henry VII was the first Tudor king: tick the phrases you think describe him best. 7 marks

generous to friends	**loving to family**	
wanted peace	**poor fighter**	**disliked music**
liked clever people	**hated his people**	**disliked money**

5. From the following list tick three women who married Henry VIII. 3 marks

Catherine of Aragon	**Anne Boleyn**
Mary of Guise	**Anne Widdecombe**
Isabella of Spain	**Alys of France**
Jane Eyre	**Jane Seymour**

Figure 5.7 Example of an examination page using minimum writing skills

assess the more complex National Curriculum levels. Specific skills such as chronology can be assessed by ordering tasks which involve simple numbering. The exam setter does have to be more innovative when setting tests for dyslexics, but this must be done in order to give them a level playing field and to ensure that you are testing their knowledge and subject skills and not penalising them for their literacy difficulties.

Study skills

Throughout this chapter the emphasis has been on developing study skills that will enable dyslexics to improve their academic performance. Not every technique will assist every pupil. The teachers' knowledge of their pupils and the subject matter being studied will determine which techniques will benefit which pupils. By mixing several techniques, a teacher will be able to provide each pupil with a range of skills that they can take with them throughout their academic career. A pupil who is confident in some skills will be confident to try to achieve more. Confidence is important for all pupils, but is particularly so for the dyslexic pupil who feels he has failed to acquire the traditional skills that will help him find success.

It is in the interests of both teacher and pupil that study skills are acquired and sustained. These techniques will speed up classroom activities and move towards easing the frustration felt by other pupils who show impatience and intolerance to their dyslexic peers. The skills will not harm any non-dyslexic pupil and can be extended, with a little imagination, to any formal area of study.

Study skills are valuable to us all at whatever level we wish to study. It is not enough for any of us to use one technique alone. We all learn differently and even those of us who are satisfied with our learning abilities are refreshed when introduced to something new. Dyslexics share the common human need for variety and stimulation. The skills discussed in this chapter may go some way towards this aim but innovation should never be discounted. New ideas are always being put forward, not least by the pupils themselves, and these should be given due consideration before being discounted. Traditional methods should not be discarded but should be operated alongside the new in order to ensure that all pupils are learning to their full potential.

6 Dyslexia and dyspraxia

Susan Flory

While not all dyslexics have problems in motor development, we find that a substantial number do. Here Susan Flory describes difficulties in gross and fine motor control, oral and visual dyspraxia, and outlines procedures on assessment and remediation.

This chapter examines the effects of dyspraxia on the daily functioning of a child within the school environment. Dyspraxia can be described as the inability to plan and carry out sequences of coordinated movements in order to achieve an objective. Having given this rather formal definition, it is helpful to illustrate the point with a reality, so let us meet 'George', a typical dyspraxic (see Figure 6.1).

George is dyspraxic. Like dyslexia, dyspraxia can affect a person in many different ways. At best, one area of functioning is impaired which does not necessarily reflect on a pupil's life and work in general and may therefore go unnoticed by his peers, although it will still have an impact on his functioning, development and attainments. At worst, like George, every aspect of day-to-day living is affected, making life difficult, disorganised and distressing.

Living life on a wobble board

Imagine being George, having problems in every area of dyspraxia. Trying to cope with the demands of daily life is like a constant battle to do what others take for granted, and achieve without too much thought and effort. It starts first thing in the morning: getting washed and cleaning teeth means coordinating the hands together and managing to squeeze the toothpaste out and onto a brush, while holding both steady. Dressing feels as if you are wearing gloves and standing on a wobble board; buttons are fiddly, ties and laces impossible, you end up with your clothes on but not quite right, so you go to breakfast feeling uncomfortable. (We have even had one boy arrive with his trousers on back to front.)

Eating breakfast is a challenge: cereal and milk from the bowl to the mouth by using a spoon over which you seem to have as much control as the knife and fork that you are expected to use to cut and pick up food (fingers are much easier but a source of disapproval). Cutting toast is also difficult so you do not bother and chocolate spread ends up all around your mouth to match the food already dropped down your clothes. Chewing is hard with the mouth closed, especially when your tongue is trying to push the food back out instead of moving it back to swallow; no one wants to sit with you to eat.

And so to school . . . but have you remembered everything that you need for the day? Assembly means trying to stand still in a small space with many people around you, concentrating and remembering all the notices that concern you.

First lesson. . . What is it?. . . Where is it?. . . Will you get there without dropping everything? Once you are there you are told to 'Sit down – Sit up', which? Work is hard, the words in your head are great but why do they rearrange themselves on the page and how did those blots get there? Your hand hurts and the pen has a mind of its own. Why is it so hard to sit on the chair, is it you or the chair that is wobbly? Then, after ten

Figure 6.1 'George', a young 'dyspraxic'

minutes your legs are hurting so you have to stand up and move to release the stress in them although you did not mean to disturb the class. Oh no! PE next, no one will pick you for their team again. So the day progresses, with this constant struggle to keep yourself and your belongings together and functioning as near to normal as you can achieve.

Not all dyspraxic pupils will exhibit this range of problems to this extent, but there are many Georges and their problems are very real and immensely obstructive to their learning and social functioning, for reasons that will be outlined in this chapter.

Meanwhile, to try to gain some understanding of and empathy with George, attempt to get dressed or write with gloves on to emulate the reduction of tactile response and the proprioceptive feedback. Also, to experience poor balance and control, try to write a dictated passage while sitting with your legs stretched out in front of you and your feet held off the floor. Notice how tiring it is, how hard to concentrate and ask yourself if that is your neatest work.

It is generally considered that about one in 12 of the population is dyspraxic; therefore a teacher can expect to have two or three pupils in a 'normal' class suffering from some aspect of dyspraxic problems. However, when co-morbidity is considered it is obvious

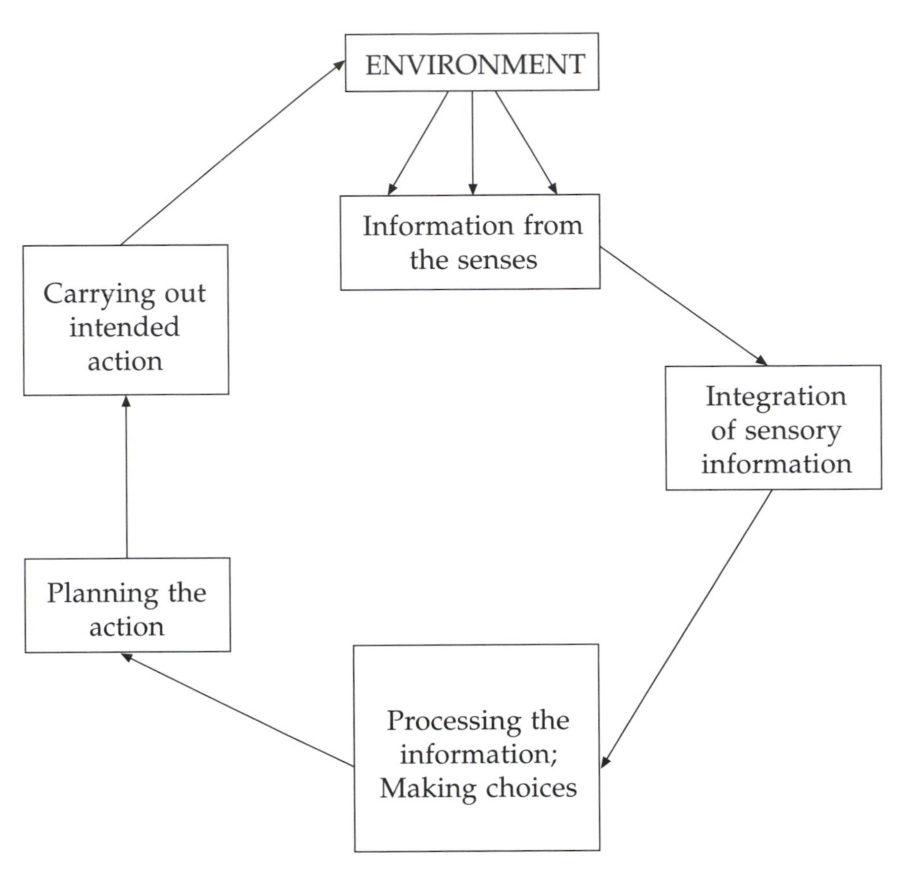

Figure 6.2 Normal efficient praxis

that children in a special unit or school are at higher risk because a dyslexic pupil or a pupil with attention deficit hyperactivity disorder is also likely to have dyspraxia.

Let us now look at some of the theoretical background to dyspraxic difficulties.

What goes wrong in dyspraxia?

Figure 6.2 illustrates how praxis is normally executed.

1. Information from the senses and their integration is poor, particularly:
   (a) vestibular – sense of balance and self in space
   (b) tactile – sense of touch and feel
   (c) propioceptive – feedback from muscles.
2. Individual actions may be achievable but the pupil may be unable to put them together into a sequence of coordinated movements to carry out the objective.
3. The pupil understands the intended sequence of movements to achieve the objective but each individual action is slow and uncoordinated.

An analogy may be asking a person to get up, cross a crowded room, open the door and leave the room, closing the door behind them. This is not a problem in normal circumstances, a sequence of actions that can be executed without conscious thought and planning.

Even a surprisingly heavy door would be negotiated. However, the same person carrying a pile of books or on crutches would have to think and plan the route and actions to successfully achieve the same objective.

The reasons why a child is affected by developmental dyspraxia (motor impairment that is not caused by another medical condition such as cerebral palsy or hemiplegia) are well documented in the publications listed as 'References and resources'. The emphasis in this chapter is on identification, assessment and remediation within the school situation.

Effects of dyspraxia

The following are tasks and activities which may cause problems.

1. *Gross motor skills* which include:
   (a) static balance – the ability to maintain steady balance and posture;
   (b) dynamic balance – the control of momentum and change of direction;
   (c) coordination – the ability to combine different actions;
   (d) perceptual-motor integration – the ability to observe and imitate a movement and fine tune with feedback from the proprioceptors.

   Lack of these skills makes integration in PE and games both in and out of class very problematic and traumatic. Muscle tone is likely to be very poor, making all activity more difficult, stamina low and improvement hard to achieve.
2. *Fine motor skills* – handwriting, drawing, model making, Lego, jigsaw puzzles etc. – all sociable activities exposing the dyspraxic to failure.
3. *Speech* – problems in making and coordinating the precise movements that are used in the production of words. It also affects the planning, organisation and sequencing of language.
4. *Feeding, eating and drinking* – difficulty using utensils, messy, fussy eater.
5. *Dressing* – untidy, inside-out, wrong way round, socks down, laces undone, dislike of tight clothing and hair being combed.
6. *Body image and body language* – poor self-awareness of own body and its position in space and in relation to other people's space. Body language gives out the wrong signals making the child a target. Lack of facial expression does not invite friendship nor does it indicate emotional state or response to learning or situations in class.
7. *Play* – inability to interpret forces required to achieve the desired movement results in upsetting peers, getting into trouble. Both this and the previous point mean that a dyspraxic child may be isolated in the playground.
8. *Organisation of self and belongings* – much time and effort is required by the dyspraxic child to get himself and his belongings to the correct place in one piece. This is because memory tends to be poor and problems with sequencing and time make a day one big confusion. A traditional timetable is of little help.
9. *Visual perception* – activities such as reading, copying and ball skills may be affected by poor control of the muscles around the eyes, the inability to cross the midline and the lack of integration of both hemispheres of the brain.
10. *Sustained control and concentration* – the inability to maintain a good sitting position for work, the need to fiddle and fidget, poor concentration and distractibility, all make learning stressful for pupil and teacher.

Parents are often the first to recognise difficulties in their child's development. Early indicators in a baby could be sleeping difficulties, fussy eater, hyperactivity, dislike of noise and touch, late reaching milestones, delayed or poor speech and little or no crawling. In a young child there could be problems in running, jumping/hopping, throwing/catching, balancing and bike riding, laterality may not be established, lack of imaginative and creative play, and poor fine motor skills.

Parents and/or professionals may well pick up these indications and dyspraxia may be diagnosed by a specialist who would provide a programme of remediation and suggestions for support within school. However, many children do go unidentified and their difficulties and behaviours put down to laziness and naughtiness. Some of the 'finer' dyspraxic problems such as visual perception, visuo-motor integration, fine motor dexterity, organisational and sequencing abilities and concentration may go unidentified and can really block a child's ability to make progress, however hard they are trying.

Screening and identification are necessary when problem areas such as any of those previously outlined are observed, or if a pupil's level of achievement is not reflected in the effort that they are making, or if they are continually failing.

In those dyslexics who have dyspraxic difficulties (ranging from mild to severe), the expected progress in their dyslexic remediation may be delayed unless their motor difficulties are addressed.

Many pupils start school with a report highlighting their problem areas, some with a programme of exercises that I will use as a basis for their help. But there are many other considerations to be addressed for their successful and happy functioning within the school situation:

- self-image and confidence
- social integration
- academic needs
- physical education needs
- day-to-day organisational skills

Identification is relatively easy for me for several reasons: many pupils coming into the school are likely to have dyspraxic difficulties, and with a whole-school approach I get valuable feedback from other members of staff. Not only do the specific reports provide valuable information, but also poor scores on performance tests (Coding, Object Assembly) on the Wechsler Intelligence Scale for Children (or similar) would be an indicator for me to 'flag up' a pupil before they start.

On the first day, the 'Georges' identify themselves; generally untidy in appearance and moving around as if tied together with string. They will find it hard to sit still in assembly and will have poor posture in class. During the first week George may well be expressing his fears about having to do games. In the gym lesson he will be a reluctant participant or will try but fail to achieve the skills that most pupils perform with comparative ease. During the first few games lessons, a series of motor skill, hand-eye and foot-eye exercises identify the pupils having problems. Then in gymnastics lessons I can identify coordination difficulties, poor stability in the shoulder and pelvic girdles and those suffering from some of the retained reflexes such as the Moro (startle) reflex. So within a very short space of time major problems have revealed themselves.

Academic staff may notice the child has problems in sitting at a desk and working, concentration or planning and organisation abilities. Care staff looking after boarders will discuss children who are not integrating at playtime or those who are having trouble with dressing and we plan ways to help them. Dining staff will highlight pupils unable to use utensils, cut and eat food easily.

I start to screen, running tests for specific things, looking initially at identified children and then at pupils who for no apparent reason are not performing to expected levels. The following general areas would be assessed:

1. Posture and anatomical well-being. The spine and feet are both common problems that are treated by our consultant osteopath/chartered physiotherapist.
2. Gross motor skills.
3. Fine motor skills.
4. Retained infantile reflexes (often the cause of the problems arising in gross and fine motor coordination, concentration and sensitivity to sound).
5. Balance.
6. Visual perception.
7. Speech, language and oral difficulties (these would normally be assessed by our speech and language therapist).

So gradually an all-round picture emerges and an action plan can be made. Many of the above will be familiar to readers but it is worth explaining some areas.

Retained infantile reflexes and their effect on motor development

In normal development there are three levels of coordination as shown in Figure 6.3, each one necessary for the building blocks upon which the next level can successfully be acquired:

Figure 6.3 Pattern of reflex and development

1. Reflexes

Babies are born with many reflexes (automatic responses to specific stimulation from their surroundings) that are important for their survival, e.g. rooting, sucking. Most of these reflexes will mature and should then disappear as development takes place. If reflexes other than those that continue to be necessary to us such as swallowing or blinking are retained, the development of gross and fine motor skills will be impeded.

2. Gross motor skills

These are large muscle movements, e.g. crawling, walking, running, which will develop into more complex coordinated movement required for skills such as throwing, skipping etc.

3. Fine motor skills

These are needed for handwriting, drawing, hand-eye coordination.

Reflexes – building blocks for development or blocking development?

Primitive reflexes emerge when the foetus is in the womb. They are vital for the process of birth and survival during the first few weeks of life when a baby is inundated by new sensations and sensory stimuli which he is not equipped to respond to with conscious thought. These reflexes are automatic, stereotyped movements directed from the brain stem with no involvement of the cortex. Each reflex emerges at a certain time, either in utero or neonatal, and is inhibited when it has served its purpose, by six months of age, or 12 months at the latest. During this time it starts to be controlled by higher centres of the brain and more sophisticated neural structures develop, allowing greater voluntary control. So it is the building block upon which more deliberate, conscious and complicated movements can be developed.

However, retained infantile or primitive reflexes may prevent the development of these more sophisticated movements, resulting in immature patterns of movement and behaviour. Known as 'aberrant reflex activity', it can account for many gross and fine muscle coordination problems found in pupils, as well as weakness in sensory perception, interpretation and understanding of information being received and expressive language; thus impairing the ability to learn.

> The fundamental equipment essential for learning will be faulty or inefficient despite adequate intellectual ability. It is as if later skills remain tethered to an earlier stage of development and instead of becoming automatic, can only be mastered through continuous conscious effort.
>
> (Goddard 1996)

An example of this would be an aberrant asymmetric tonic neck reflex. This reflex is evident in a baby to develop the ability to reach out and grasp that which is seen with the eyes; as the head turns towards an object there is an automatic outward movement of the arm on that side of the body, the primary development of hand-eye coordination. The retention of this means that a pupil who is sitting working and turns the head to look at the book or worksheet to one side of the desk, has an involuntary movement in the arm resulting in poor writing. (In extreme cases there may also be stresses and movements down the legs.) Very cleverly, the body may try to compensate for this by strongly fixing around the shoulders and down the arms, making the effort of writing very tense and tiring. So we see that retained reflexes can become a block to learning rather than a building block. Research by Bender (1971) indicates that approximately 75 per cent of children with learning disabilities have an immature symmetric tonic neck reflex as a contributing factor.

Detection of retained reflexes is most important. This needs to be done by someone trained to screen for them, and will include symmetric tonic neck, asymmetric tonic neck, spinal gallant, Moro and labyrinth reflexes. Then an appropriate programme of exercises has to be devised that will first mature and, as a consequence, inhibit the reflexes. A programme should include patterns of movement based on those that would have been done as an infant and would need to be done daily for a period of nine to 12 months. Results can be dramatic, as the following example shows.

Pupil X came to East Court for his dyslexia. He was coping well in games and gymnastics and any difficulties had not come to my notice within the first few weeks of term. However, his typing tutor asked me to have a look at him, as he seemed unable to sit and type, preferring to stand. During a discussion with X he told me that after about five to ten minutes of sitting down to work his legs hurt and he had to get up to relieve the stress. He made no fuss, just worked standing up. Putting him through some screening tests revealed that he had a very strong symmetric tonic neck reflex and an asymmetric tonic neck reflex that were retained. He was given a small alarm to use in certain classes that would remind him to stand up to relieve the stress before it affected him. He was started on a programme that included commando crawling, creeping (crawling on hands and knees), rocking backwards and forwards in a particular manner, and head turning. Within a matter of months pupil X was feeling much more comfortable and was able to sit and work for a whole lesson.

Although the retention of reflexes has a profound effect on the development of more complex, voluntary movements, pupils with developmental dyspraxia can learn new skills. However, their acquisition is more difficult and takes longer. More practice is needed to achieve a functional level of skill and this is often not transferred to other learning situations where the skills needed might be the same or similar.

Checking laterality: hand/foot/eye/ear

Once the absence or presence of reflexes is established, an assessment of motor development must take place. Here, the teacher can observe a pupil's ability to perform certain tasks and any 'sympathetic' movements being made in the hands or face. By allowing the pupil to choose the foot or hand to use in a task laterality, dominance or confusion can be recorded. The areas listed in Table 6.1 may be assessed:

This type of screening will identify specific difficulties and give areas that can be worked on to improve efficiency of movement and coordination and are a useful measure of dyspraxia and improvements made. However, it does not show the day-to-day effects that the problem has on a pupil.

Table 6.1 Assessing gross motor skills

Ask child to:	*Note:*
General static/balance	
Standing straight and then	Check position, feet, knees, spine, shoulders, head for postural problems
With eyes closed	Ability to maintain stable position without visual input
Lying straight, curl/return to straight Lying star shape, curl/return to star shape	These exercises show a knowledge of the body in space. Curl and back to the original position with accuracy of position
Stand on tiptoes – 10 secs.	
Balance on one foot and then balance on other	Observe preferred foot and timing on each (30 seconds is 'norm')
Balance on one foot with eyes closed then balance on other foot with eyes closed	Observe preferred foot
General motor	
Walk and run forwards and backwards	General ease of movement Note any arm flapping
Run around changing direction	
Run and stop on command	Control of body weight
Walk on tiptoes, heels, outsides of feet, insides of feet	Note any sympathetic movement of hands
Walk heel to toe (pigeon steps)	Accurate placing of heel to toe
Knowledge of body parts	Ability to touch when part named
Shrug shoulders	A dyspraxic may not be able to isolate arms, will also flex the elbows
Dynamic motor and coordination	
Hop on one foot, then on the other	Note the choice of foot, lightness of action
Jump with two feet together	Watch for ability to keep feet together, arm flapping
Star jumps, step ups	Note dominant foot and coordination
Skip, hopscotch	
Jump over rope 20cm 30cm 40cm	Note dominant foot
Jump trampette	Watch the control of body in the air, arm flapping
Log roll, both directions	Ability to roll in a straight line
Commando crawl	Arms and legs in opposition, head still
Creeping	Feet flat on floor, back straight, head up, hands facing forwards and flat

Gross motor skills – problem areas

- Lack of body awareness both of self and self in space.
- Poor muscle tone, therefore an inability to control movement and maintain good posture.
- Lack of stamina and general lethargy, will not be able to maintain levels of physical output and likely to be inactive in the playground thus not improving muscle tone.
- Lack of control of body weight and speed when stopping or changing direction, creating problems when playing games.
- Little or no sense of balance (bike riding, skateboarding).
- Dizziness when turning the head quickly.
- Little sense of force, leading to problems of touch and play with peers.

- Inability to carry out a sequence of movements.
- Poor sense of rhythm and timing.
- Lack of coordination for activities such as skipping.
- Lack of experience of the body in different positions leading to fear and no knowledge of where the body parts are and how to move them, making many gymnastic skills a very great challenge.
- Inability to maintain body stillness, apparent inattentiveness.
- Over-excitable and impulsive attitude to learning, distracting and easily distracted.

There are many implications here for both the learning situation and social integration. With the knowledge that he is likely to fail, it is no surprise that the dyspraxic child avoids physical activity. He experiences rejection, even ridicule. With careful handling of situations, understanding of the child's problems and a depth of knowledge of the material, the teacher can help the child to achieve many skills and enable him to take part in PE and games lessons and play socially.

- Give lots of varied experience, a little at a time, often, achievable and make it fun.
- Break down skills into simple manageable components. Even the most complex movement like a cartwheel is achievable when presented in smaller steps.
- Give verbal cues: 'be ready and steady', 'watch the ball', 'step, hop – step, hop'.
- Give physical cues, e.g. touch the leg or arm that needs to be used. Help the child move his body through the movement or part of it to 'feel' the pattern.
- Avoid children choosing teams or control this carefully.
- Help the child be aware of other people's space and improve their ability to control their touch.

Activities to help with the development of gross motor skills

- **Body awareness:** Games naming and identifying body parts such as 'Simon Says', partner work imitating movement, using pictures to imitate body positions and move from one to another.
- **Muscle tone:** Lots of fun activities with challenges, jumping on a trampoline or trampette, step-ups, pulling along a bench, crouch jumps, bunny hops etc.
- **Control of body weight:** Running forwards, backwards, sideways, fast/slow, stop/start, changing direction on command, learning to use all muscles in the body (particularly the abdomen) to support the body in movement and stillness.
- **Balance:** Use of wobble boards, large physio balls to develop the ability to correct the body weight in balance; train the pupil to use a focal point when balancing and the muscles in the torso and legs to aid balance by 'pulling up'; use equipment such as upturned benches to walk along to gain confidence, techniques and experience; head-turning and body-circling activities to improve the function of the vestibular system.
- **Sequencing:** Games gradually building up the ability to remember a sequence, e.g. Catch the ball, throw back . . . clap, catch the ball, throw back . . . clap, catch the ball, turn around, throw back. . . etc. Matching partner work.
- **Spatial awareness:** Moving around apparatus, under and through without touching it. Moving around with other pupils without touching or bumping, stopping in front of others and leaving enough space.
- **Rhythm:** Clapping games, clapping and moving, action songs, rhythmical actions such as star jumps, marching, skipping.
- **Crossing the midline:** Cross crawl and 'Lazy Eights' (Brain Gym), picking up and throwing things across the body, juggling, symmetric and asymmetric movements.
- **Kinaesthetic sense:** Beanbags, different weight and size balls to catch from teacher/self, to throw back or into or at a target, to kick and dribble learning different forces required.

Activities should be achievable so that the pupils can feel good about themselves, building up confidence in themselves and the teacher. It is easy to give a pupil his own 'special challenge'.

The last point made here about the kinaesthetic sense is interesting. It may not be realised how much we rely on our physical knowledge of how a movement or action feels. Imagine having to think about what sequence of movement is required every time you wanted to change gear when driving. To gain a little insight into how much this sense helps us to achieve tasks easily and how hard it is when there is little or no sense, try the following test. Close your eyes and write your name and address with your preferred hand. This will no doubt look not dissimilar to your normal writing; you know how it feels to write these familiar words and the movement is 'programmed' into your hand. Now close your eyes and do the same but with your other hand. Notice how much harder you have to try, how awkward it feels and how stressful it is. When you have no kinaesthetic sense, work is much harder: preparing to do a vault in gym or a high jump in athletics is so much more daunting when you cannot remember how it is going to feel and therefore how to fine tune the action during performance.

Table 6.2 Assessing fine motor skills

Ask child to:		*Note:*
Touch finger to nose		Eyes closed, the ability to touch tip of nose
Finger touching (left or right hand)	one / other / both	Touching of fingers successively with thumb
Bead threading		Coordinating two hands efficiently
Peg board, putting pegs into a board	one	As with above activities, note dominant hand
	other	Watch for correct pincer use of thumb and forefinger
	both	Coordination of the two hands
Brick tower		As above
Catch		Using different size/weight balls
Throw		Accuracy of direction and distance
Catch/throw to self		Need more control and coordination, do eyes focus?
Kick ball		Note dominant foot

Fine motor skills – problem areas

The assessment of fine motor skills is shown in Table 6.2.

- **Handwriting:** This may be illegible or untidy, too heavy, too spidery, poorly set out on the page. Pen/pencil often held in an immature grip, posture poor due to aberrant reflexes, head trying to stabilise other arm. (Examples are given in Figures 6.4 and 6.5. Note in particular in Figure 6.5 the discrepancy between the handwritten plan and the word processed essay, and how this affects the reader's judgement.)
- **Drawing:** The same problems occur as in writing.
- **Eating:** Unable to hold utensils in the conventional manner as well as coordinating them to cut up food and get the food to the mouth. The action of eating may also be affected (see 'Oral dyspraxia and its effects' below).
- **Dressing:** Lack of feedback from the muscles and tactile senses makes manipulating buttons and doing them up difficult and takes longer. Clothes are put on inside out, back to front, left undone.
- **Use of scissors:** The coordination of the cutting action as well as the two hands together to achieve neat incisions is very hard.
- **Games:** Any game requiring hand/eye coordination such as Lego, jigsaw puzzles, construction kits, is usually avoided.
- **Laterality:** Often a confusion of dominance, right for some things but left for others, right-handed and left-footed etc. This may mean that the dominant side of the brain is not being used or activated, there may be a delay because of transferring information. Occasionally a child will actually choose the worst foot to try to perform an action.

- **Facial expression:** Some dyspraxic children have very passive faces, giving no clues as to how they are feeling or responding in class. More importantly, they do not invite friendship because they give out the wrong signals.
- **Oral skills:** If the fine muscles controlling the mouth, lips and tongue (see below) are affected then chewing, swallowing and the production and control of sound may all be impaired.
- **Visual skills:** The fine controlling muscles around the eyes, if not working effectively (see below), can impair the ability to follow text.

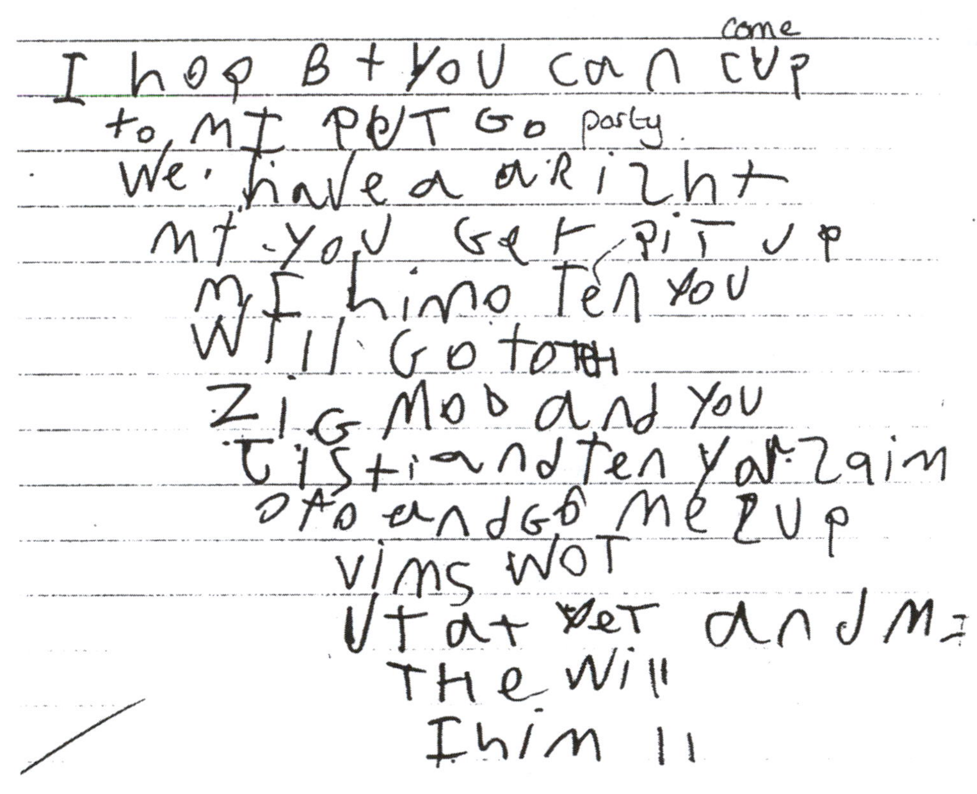

Figure 6.4 Example of work (12 years old) showing poor writing and setting out

Help for fine motor skills in the school situation

- Maturing and inhibiting the symmetric and asymmetric tonic neck reflexes.
- Individual lessons for specific skills, for example, handwriting lessons – specific methods and equipment; art lessons – support and tasks to improve weak skills; games lessons – cues and adapted equipment to aid success; drama lessons – exercises to improve facial expression.
- Use of specific equipment and games to improve strength in fingers/hands, fine manipulation and coordination used in lessons and in leisure time.
- Eye exercises to improve the muscles.
- Crossword puzzles, dot-to-dot and spot the difference puzzles.

Helpful aids, materials and games

- Use large paper and felt-tip pens to develop control, shape and then letter forms, graduating to smaller paper and pencil/pen as control is gained. A sloped surface is beneficial, as are pencil triangles to assist grip.
- Pegs can be used to gain 'pincer' grip for correct pencil hold.
- Finger games such as Flick Football, finger puppets, finger rhymes.
- Peg boards, bead threading, building bricks, size according to age and ability, Lego etc.

- Games requiring control, e.g. Jacks, Pick-up Sticks, Tiddly Winks, as well as Plasticine, play dough, clay modelling.
- Piano playing.
- Picking up small things like rice to develop the use of thumb and forefinger.
- Screwing and unscrewing lids and squeezy balls to develop strength in the hands.
- Specialist scissors.
- Blu-Tack on ruler to hold it in position.
- Cat's cradle.

Oral dyspraxia and its effects

Dyspraxia can also affect muscles in the mouth and cause problems with feeding, eating and drinking. If the muscles in the mouth are not working and responding normally, a child may not develop the correct feeding patterns.

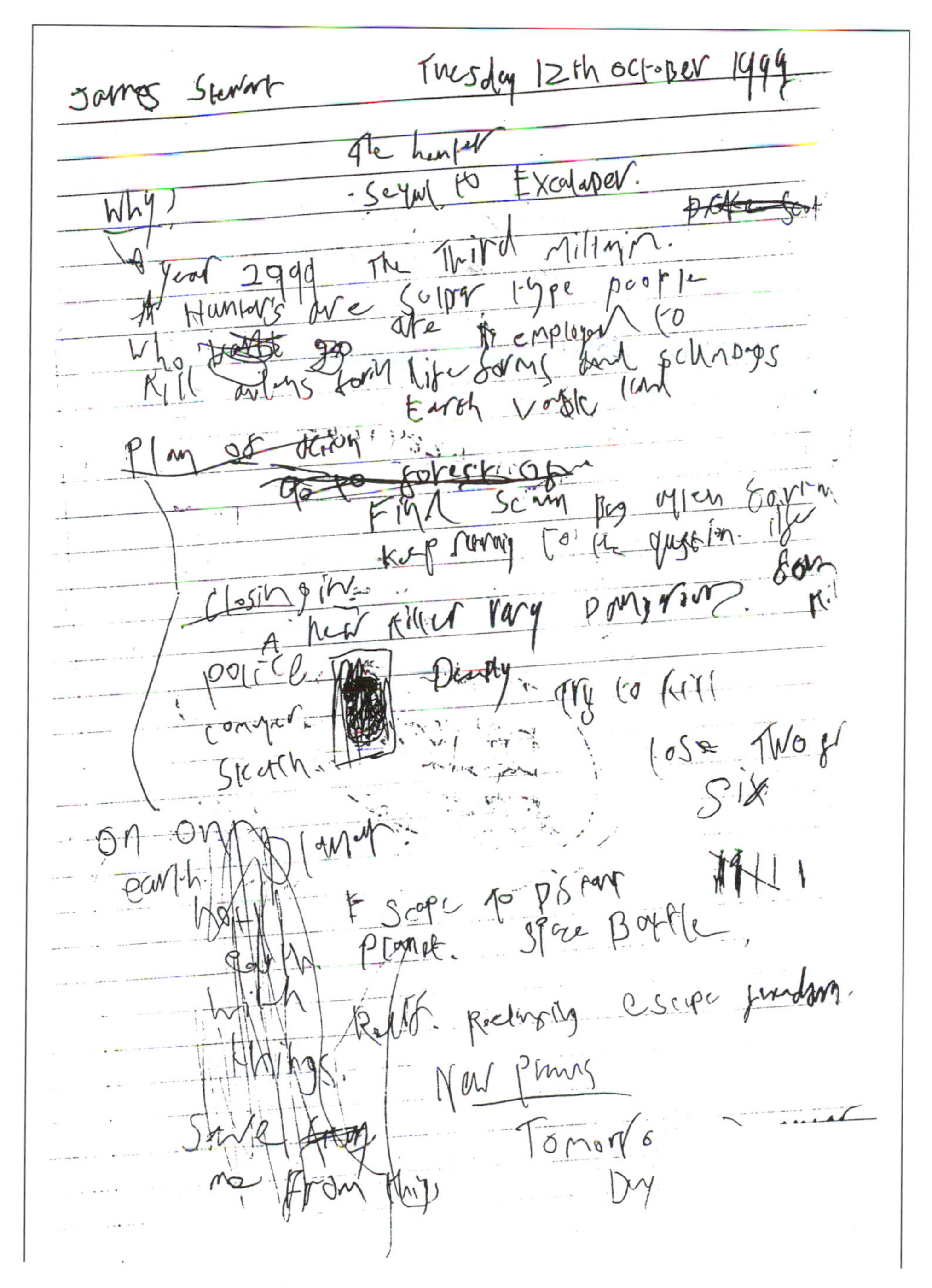

James Stewart Tuesday 12th October 1999

The Hunter

Some hunt to eat, others hunt for sport, I hunt to save the good people of the world from death. I am a hunter, a person who hunts down criminals, the phrase bounty hunter is not associated with us. We only work for the police. The world ran out of natural resources in the year 50,000 there is only one city it is called Happy-town, but it was far from it, Happy-town was crowded with people it was so small if some one shouted everyone would hear it. A City with the name of a town it just keeps on getting weirder. armour

I picked up my body armor it was six inches thick camouflage panels on the top. I picked up my exterminator gun it was about the size of as a child of three years of age. It weighed the amount of a table. I laid the strap of my gun on my back. It was so heavy. Next I lifted a backpack full of weapons and placed it on my back. I put on my helmet and I was ready.
"All right then you lot get in line and shout when I call your name." Said the sergeant.
"Drick!" the sergeant belowed.
"Sir." bellowed.
"Peat!"
"Sir."
"stronsun"
Strongson let out a long scream and then span around like he was mad he was the class clown.
"Get in rank man!"
The sergeant ticked off his name.
"Stewart!"
"Sir!" I shouted.
"I'm only here Stewart!" Said the sergeant.
"Right boys illegal use of Androids and Drugs! Please for goodness sake boys make it a clean one."
And as soon as that last decibel was said we all ran to the van.
"I hate killing." I said. I was the only one out of the group who had never killed anyone or anything.
"You excited?" A guy next to me asked.

Figure 6.5 One pupil's essay handwritten and word-processed

Normally a baby develops from sucking and swallowing to squash and swallow, chew with teeth, use of tongue to move food back to swallow. A child may not develop further than squash and swallow, which will mean that they will be a fussy eater who only likes food that can be eaten easily. Muscles can be developed by giving the child some very specific help. Take Pupil Y who had a 'tongue thrust': as he put food into his mouth he wanted to chew and swallow but his tongue was wanting to push it out. We encouraged the muscles to respond correctly by giving him thick yoghurt to suck through a straw, bread to chew and blow pens to 'paint' pictures. Within a very short time he was able to sit and eat with his peers without them complaining about his eating habits.

- Oral dyspraxia may also cause problems such as dribbling, nasal resonance and runny nose. Many dyspraxic children have to be taught to blow their noses. There can be

problems with fluency of speech, including problems in sequencing of sounds, control of breathing and phonation, prosody – intonation, stress patterns and rhythm with which words are said, control of volume, often speak too loudly.
- Listening and attention skills may also be affected, including a dislike of loud noise and being easily distracted by sound.
- Verbal dyspraxia can result in slow language development, affecting comprehension, length of sentence, grammatical forms and word retrieval. The language of time, space and self-awareness, as well as social skills, response to questions/instructions, facial expressions and the ability to express feelings, may all be affected.
- Poor language development may be substituted by physical behaviour to achieve results. The behaviour may be punished but the cause is not addressed.
- An ability to express feelings through speech as well as facial expression and body language attracts response and friendship. Children with passive faces give out the wrong signals and are unable to read those of other people. They are at risk of social rejection; they will be the children on their own in the far part of the playground.
- Non-reaction to an instruction may not be defiance but an inability to understand.

Visual dyspraxia/perception

Problems that may be exhibited include:

- reluctance to read more than a few lines or as the print gets smaller; omitting words or lines;
- looking up regularly to rest the eyes;
- rubbing the eyes or shaking the head as if to correct eyes or screwing up or covering one eye;
- turning the head to one side;
- watery or red eyes after reading;
- inability to track along a line and/or cross the midline;
- inability to see patterns and shapes;
- poor observation for drawing;
- poor spatial ability in setting out work;
- avoidance of jigsaw puzzles and perceptual games.

Pupils can be helped by:

- use of enlarged text;
- use of line guide on text;
- bar magnifier;
- paired reading;
- copy from paper not board;
- marks on paper as guides for writing/drawing;
- use of exercises/games/equipment to improve perceptual skills;
- tracking, 'Lazy Eights' and focus exercises;
- coloured overlays.

Figure 6.6 shows work from three pupils, all aged 13 years and who have all received the same teaching input and support. It is not hard to see that one pupil has significant visual perception problems.

Remediation and intervention – summary

Identify which areas of functioning are affected by dyspraxia and prioritise:

- functioning in the classroom;
- social interaction;

- organisation;
- other problems identified by parents, teachers, pastoral helpers.

Establish any:

- visual problems that can be treated by an ophthalmologist;
- hearing difficulties;
- retained primitive reflexes;
- anatomical problems which need osteopathic treatment;
- oral dyspraxia for treatment by the speech therapist;
- other areas of dysfunction.

With all the available information a programme of remediation can be worked out and implemented. Remediation should take place:

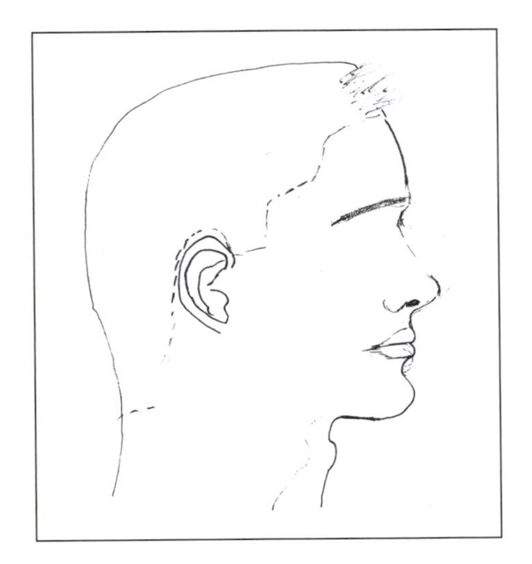

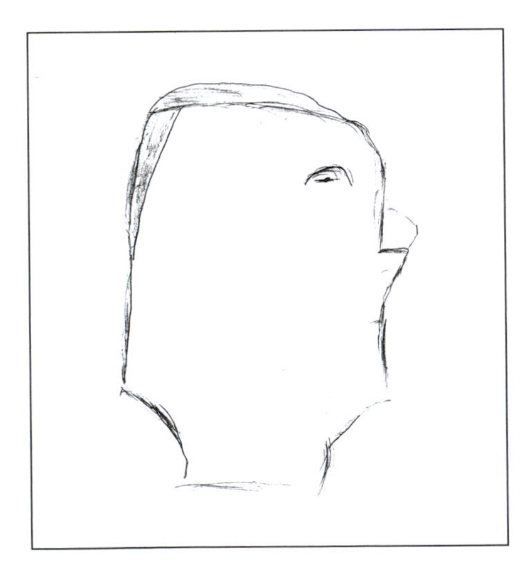

Figure 6.6 Examples of art work by three 13 year-old students in the same lesson

- in individual sessions addressing the specific needs – for many, on a daily basis, especially where aberrant reflexes are involved;
- in PE/games lessons, where skills are adapted and broken down into achievable steps; equipment and rules are adapted to enable integration; emphasis is on personal development rather than competitiveness;
- as a whole-school approach with all teachers aware of individual problems, needs and help that can be given; care staff with a knowledge of what to look for in identifying

problems and how to support the individual in the everyday living and social aspects of school life;
- with home involvement – this is most important for continuity and understanding.

Within the school, and to some extent at home, it may be necessary to consider the following points to avoid mobility problems and annoying others:

- where the pupil sits in class
- where their bed is in the dormitory
- their position at the dining table.

Supply and adapt equipment as discussed in previous sections:

- a sloped board for writing
- pencil grip
- large print books
- photocopies instead of copying from the board
- different equipment in games
- equipment that can be attached to school folder to avoid dropping
- visual/colour-coded timetable to help with organisation.

Give visual, verbal and physical clues in early stages.
Teach new skills in achievable steps.
Teach coping strategies.
Encourage asking for help and saying when things are difficult.
Help with dressing by:

- Cannot tie shoe laces – use Velcro fastenings and teach lace tying.
- Right/left confusion – mark shoes in a way the child can understand.
- Use labels to aid getting things the correct way round.
- If possible allow more time for dressing/changing and enough space to avoid bumping into others, muddling and losing things.

Most of all, be patient and praise them when they get things right for themselves. Help them to get off the wobble board and live life with greater ease and success.

7 A counsellor's perspective on dyslexia

Rosemary Scott

Dyslexia is primarily a cognitive learning difficulty but it has implications for how the dyslexics feel about themselves and the effects on their families. In this final chapter Rosemary Scott reviews these issues and discusses them from a counselling perspective. Dr Scott's book on the subject is due out in 2003.

Ring the bells that still can ring
Forget your perfect offering
There is a crack in everything
That's how the light gets in
Leonard Cohen

As a counsellor of dyslexic children, students and adults, my experience is that dyslexic clients have distinctive characteristics all of their own. For example, their information processing delays, short-term memory deficit, irregular perceptions of time and sequencing can give an alarming spin to appointment keeping and communication. Their 'out of the box' view of the world, their creativity, eccentricity, kinaesthetic and visual approach to identifying and solving their problems have invigorated my way of working in the more verbal world of counselling. I have also found that there are some common factors behind the problems in the dyslexic experience that trip up dyslexic people in certain idiosyncratic ways. I propose that a non-dyslexic person will be better placed to read dyslexic behaviour if they are aware of these factors, and how they have contributed to the dyslexic world view.

School

Problems with dyslexia start, although by no means end, with school. Without school, dyslexics would be as trouble-free as they were in a preliterate, agricultural society where their skills would have made them valuable artisans or engineers. I expect that in a computer-dominated, post-literate future, dyslexia will become an asset again. For now, however, a literacy-based society does not favour dyslexia, and school, the engine of literacy, is still the slowly tightening hell a dyslexic child has to face every single day. It is school that must take principal responsibility for changing normal children, who just happen to be dyslexic, into the shrunken balls of misery or sullen, angry individuals who watch helplessly as their mysterious affliction – dyslexia – blocks out the sun of success, friendship and optimism.

Putting it more directly, dyslexic people have been – and still are – traumatised by their experiences at school. I have seen adult dyslexic clients, of all ages, distraught as they relive the terror of their long morning journey to school and the psychological torture of the long day to follow. One elderly client succumbed to a full panic attack whenever she visualised the moment when she arrived at the school gate as a nine-year-old girl. Last year, a brilliant 23-year-old chemistry postgraduate wept uncontrollably through most of a one-hour session as he recalled beatings and bullying through the endless failures of his elementary school.

School can infect the dyslexic boy or girl with viruses of frustration, anger and fear that are so potent that they can still be raging even half a century later. To my mind, there are two broad ways in which this is done – failure and bullying.

Failure at school

Dyslexics can fail in so many ways. Principally, at school, they fail to read and write, and this is a very public failure. It is experienced every time a dyslexic is asked to act on written instructions, read aloud or read anything at all – events which happen dozens of times every school day. Failure must also be anticipated at every examination and at every reading of test results. Many of my dyslexic clients find it traumatic to recall the anticipatory terror around these simple events and recount the desperate strategies they devised of avoiding them. Some can still vividly taste their fear, and clearly remember their intense shame and embarrassment among the sniggers and jeers of the rest of the class.

Yet there are other types of failure at school. For a dyslexic, failure to make friends is one of the most painful, and any failure to gain peer approval can have a lasting effect well into adult life, and is a major contributor to adolescent and adult depression. Much of this problem has to do with the aetiology of bullying, but it is also true that dyslexic children can be cut off from peer interaction through poor social skills. For example, dyslexic children have problems with information processing delay so, in conversation, they can still be furiously unpacking one lot of information while their peers have moved several sentences down the line. The blank look that accompanies this perusal of incoming data is off-putting. It can make a dyslexic person seem uncommunicative, or even slightly 'simple', and discourages the rapid to-and-fro of chat which bonds a peer group.

Dyspraxia also adds its own type of failure. Eating can be a messy process for children with dyspraxic difficulties, and such children can end up with food over them, the table and their fellow eaters, with eating utensils going every which way. Even the most tolerant of children can find this process disgusting to see and can express this revulsion dramatically and publicly (see Chapter 6). Additionally, although it is true that some dyslexics do excel and achieve success at sport, for many their clumsiness, lack of coordination and poor sports skills can add up to even more failure outside the classroom, and many dyslexic children are left out of play activity by their peers and politely passed over in sports teams by teachers.

There are also hundreds of other daily, small failures and opportunities for belittlement that can litter the lives of dyslexics. Problems with sequencing and perception of time can mean that dyslexic children fail to get to class, or they may go through the wrong sequence of doors to fetch up in some terrifying no-man's-land. Illiteracy means that they cannot read signs so, when they do get lost, they can't find their own way out. Timetables and instructions may as well be in Chinese, while clumsiness and fine motor coordination problems lead to frequent tripping over dangling shoelaces and trails of dropped paper from files. Memory problems translate into lost work, forgotten deadlines, jobs half done and mislaid books, laptops and briefcases. Carefully prepared examinations are missed. This social image is neither a successful nor an elegant one, and dyslexic children know it.

Bullying

Dyslexic children have a high chance of being bullied by both teachers and peers. A survey at East Court showed that 80 per cent had been bullied at previous schools, some of them several times every day.

Bullying, with its connotations of 'jolly japes', can be, in reality, severe emotional, physical or sexual assault, which the dyslexic child cannot escape. Dyslexic children have described themselves as 'bullied' when they have been, variously, half-drowned in lavatories, sprayed with lighter fluid and set alight, had an arm slowly twisted and broken by a group of boys as an adult observed and did not intervene (somehow he found this the worst part of the experience), and regaled daily with phrases such as 'spastic cunt', 'lazy, stupid fucker', 'dyslexic turd'.

Teachers have made their own contributions by tearing up long-toiled-over work and dispensing both public classroom humiliation and physical assault. In recent years, I have heard of dyslexic children being hurled around the classroom, pelted with objects, beaten and verbally eviscerated and, only this year, a 12-year-old boy wrote of being caned repeatedly in a French school when he made spelling mistakes. Gentler forms of abuse can also destroy dyslexic children. One of the most school traumatised children I have ever counselled was a painfully sensitive boy who could not bear the daily calm rebukes and expressed disappointment from a teacher he adored and wanted to please above all else.

Undoubtedly, bullying is a complex phenomenon, and several reasons have been advanced for why dyslexic children are disproportionately at its receiving end. There may be reasons in a dyslexic child's family dynamics, something I consider significant and shall discuss in more detail below. There is also the self-fulfilling prophesy whereby dyslexic children, because of their poor peer relationships, low self-esteem, poor social skills, clumsiness, destroyed confidence and general bewilderment, present with classic victim characteristics to which other children are only too willing to respond, especially if teachers are leading the way. This 'victim' behaviour can then become entrenched. I shall also return to this later.

Family

Dyslexic children are keenly aware that they are failing their parents. They know that they are a disappointment. Both parents – but particularly the successful, academic, non-dyslexic fathers – make it quite clear to their dyslexic child how stupid, lazy and thick they believe him to be. What dyslexic children also pick up is the accurate suspicion that their parents are bereaved; that their mum and dad have lost the perfect, successful and untroubled child that they thought they had – at least until that perfect child went to school.

Children are programmed to please adults, especially their mum and dad. Dyslexic children, more so before diagnosis, have to face the fact that, for some utterly inexplicable reason and despite some often herculean effort, their parents are not at all pleased with what they do and who they are. Very quickly, this becomes the horrific conviction that their parents' love may well be conditional on the one thing that, try as they might, they cannot provide; that is, any measurable literacy. It is a very common belief among dyslexic children that continued academic failure will lead them to lose their parents' love, and this belief is recalled, often as a painful certainty, by dyslexic adults.

Dyslexic children also feel considerable guilt – at the trouble they cause; for failing to be a more desirable child; at the energy, money and worry their parents expend on them. They also feel guilt at the hatred they feel, and often secretly indulge, towards a younger sibling who reads and spells so much better than they can, and who is admired in ways that they never are. Like rats in a maze, dyslexic children also have no exit option. They find that refusing to go to school, trying – by any means – to stay at home, gets them hell from their parents, but going to school gives them hell for themselves. That most dyslexic children still persist in attending school despite this odious choice is a measure both of their dignity and character, and their love for, and desire to please, their parents.

When I counsel the families of dyslexic children, I find a number of subtle parental politics into which dyslexic children can get sucked. For example, I have counselled dyslexic children who have become the family scapegoat, accepting in the family politic the scorn of siblings and parents and, eventually, internalising all the 'bad' things in the family. Also, not at all uncommon is the family where the dyslexic father wants his son to get the help that he was denied, and then resents his son for receiving the help that he did not. Such a father can also find, and dislike, in his son the daily, unbearable reminder of his own failure as a child.

The dyslexic child can also get caught up in the parental relationship. I have often encountered the situation where a mother anxiously and guiltily overprotects her dyslexic child, to the envy and resentment of her husband, something that becomes much worse if the father is dyslexic himself and did not have his own mother's support. This fight over the mother/wife's attention, this acting out of very complex relationships, often leads to marital break-up for which the dyslexic child can feel responsible, and adds to his burden of guilt.

Overprotective parenting can also be powered by latent and unexpressed feelings of dislike, disappointment or even hatred that the mother or father feels towards an excruciatingly problematic dyslexic child. Unfortunately, this incongruent reaction – which the child can pick up on but not explain or discuss – has two effects. Firstly, it can make him anxious and, secondly, the overprotection itself, by implicitly suggesting that he cannot manage alone, is disempowering and adds both to the increased probability of bullying at school and the encouragement of a victim self-image. Unfortunately, in this situation, the dyslexic child starts to show even more dependence, anxiety and neediness, the very behaviours that the mother, and particularly the father, may so dislike but cannot express.

Not unrelated to this is the scenario where the child's dyslexia gives the mother an excuse to avoid separation. In this case, the mother can find ways in which her dyslexic child is rewarded for remaining helpless and failed, since his success renders her redundant. Such mothers can resist help for their dyslexic child, or even sabotage it. This situation is also made worse when the mother herself is dyslexic, since she may be acting out her own feelings of failure and, often, the inability of her own mother to help her. She can create her own fantasised ending to what she had wanted for herself.

As a footnote to this, and to complete the circle, it is notable that research in other fields suggests that this last scenario is also significant in school refusal. Additionally, the parental model of overprotective, anxious mother and aggressive, resentful father, often found among dyslexic children, is also shown, independently, to be linked to higher probabilities of a child being bullied.

Some behavioural effects of dyslexia

I have picked out for discussion four areas, which I have found to be common effects among dyslexic people of the types of experiences outlined above.

Anxiety, stress and defences

Dyslexia, stress and anxiety are, to my mind, co-related. I have never yet met a dyslexic who has not been under stress for most of his life, or has not manifested some variant of anxiety-related disorder. If it is not the stress of pressure – either to avoid failure or find success – then it is that of boredom, of shoehorning a gallon of intellect and ability into pint pots of menial jobs and low expectations.

This stress and anxiety are the direct and indirect response to actual and anticipated failure, fear, frustration, suppressed anger and the erosion of confidence. Coping with these feelings, literally finding ways of staying sane and cheerful, lead, I propose, to two broad categories of psychological defence among dyslexic clients: outer and inner.

Outer defences

In the case of dyslexic people who use outer defences, everything is out there and in your face. From classrooms to pubs, they are defiant and extrovert. They grab attention before someone or something can grab them. Sarcastic, witty and aggressive, such dyslexics can also dress and behave to divert or alarm. I remember some markedly biting, demanding counselling with two fierce and fascinating dyslexic clients – one a huge 19-year-old student, the other a diminutive ten-year-old boy – who were both so covered in chains, tattoos, leather, studs, their hair in angry hedgehog spikes, that it was obvious that only a brave person would dare to try anything with them, let alone get close. Other outer-directed dyslexics can be very funny indeed, or use a charm offensive with such stunning effect that the observer is quite captivated. All these strategies are used principally to deflect attention from any potential failure or criticism.

Others – often girls – become so over-adapted to the needs of others that they have acquired huge, invisible radar dishes that enable them to be and do exactly what they think you want. Such dyslexics can be so superb and subtle at this that it is easy not to notice their low self-esteem and the lack of any identity of their own. By contrast, there is the aggressive, charmless, 'don't care what you think' defence, which conceals the huge anxiety of someone who cares very much indeed. With all these types of outer defence, the deal is that you get lost in the smoke screen of their behaviour and do not notice the failure and vulnerability beneath.

A more active outer defence is the attempt to revisit earlier problems and solve them in the safety of adulthood. There are, for example, many dyslexic, mature students who decide, with considerable courage, that they can only lay the stressful ghosts of their childhood by going back and facing them. It is as if they want to gain some retrospective control over their childhood misery. They also want to prove finally to themselves and others that 'they can do it'. The ways chosen by these dyslexic adults can be extraordinarily difficult, and occasionally unwise. For example, dyslexic students often choose to study such book-infested and language-dominated subjects as English, philosophy, social sciences and psychology. Such is the outstanding degree of their motivation that these students are often successful. Sometimes, however, I do need, as a counsellor, to challenge the enormous anxiety such decisions can cause.

One dyslexic client, a talented, intelligent artist who was barely literate, insisted on studying Psychology A level. After two weeks of incomprehension and sleeplessness, we were able to look at the issue of choice. Did he now, as an adult, have to do it? Could he not now give himself the options that his parents did not? Did he need such an extreme defence for his childhood failures? Could he now find value in who he was rather than who he thought he had to be or – importantly – who his father wanted him to be?

Finally, other obvious outer defences revolve around drugs and alcohol which are common solutions to reducing anxiety. Of the dyslexic clients who come to counselling – some as young as 13 – a significant proportion want to beat their addiction to tobacco, cocaine, marijuana, Ecstasy and all types of drink. Some dyslexics want to solve the problems that have led to their long-standing use of antidepressants.

Among children I have, surprisingly, rarely encountered anorexia among dyslexic girls. More common is bulimia, which often represents some need to exert personal control for the sufferer. I have, on the other hand, encountered more under-eating problems among male dyslexic children and adult students which – since anorexia is now seen as a function of incongruence in family relationships – may reflect a male dyslexic's need to exert control against family pressure.

In some ways, I find the outer defences reassuring. At least the anger and resentment are out there and not festering within, and both humour and charm can give the dyslexic a sense of control and success which are important first steps to self-esteem.

Inner defences

Inner defences are much more worrying. These are found in dyslexic clients who have either given up or gone so far inside themselves that they have forgotten the route back to the self they once were. This group presents with clinical depression, panic attacks, self-harm, anxiety disorders – including obsession – and is also the group at greatest risk of suicide attempts and nervous breakdown. Since research has long shown that peer rejection and bullying are statistically linked to both child and adult depression, it is also unsurprising that so many dyslexic children and adults present in counselling with these symptoms.

At this point, I must note that no dyslexic adult or child can be counselled if they are sufficiently detached or depressed, and sometimes medication with this group must be a first step. Although it may seem a desperate measure, I have seen Prozac prescribed to significant, positive effect with a number of children – some as young as nine – particularly where the presenting anxiety disorder takes an obsessive-compulsive flavour.

In this inner-defended group, a typical adult client has been the highly intelligent, driven, sensitive person who has always overworked to keep pace and, somehow, always succeeded. They have, for many years, bumped along under the line marked 'full' on their anxiety tanks. Going over the 'full' mark inevitably and catastrophically leads to breakdown. The difference between managing and not managing is absolute.

Another inner defence used by dyslexic clients, particularly children, is the ability to go deeply inside themselves to a world of fantasy where the distressing, outer world is excluded. In these wonderful sanctuaries, dyslexic children are powerful, successful and drive their enemies (teachers, other children, sisters, brothers) to various imaginative forms of destruction. Such children are disassociated, deadened and dreamy in a way comparable to the behaviour presented by victims of child abuse.

In effect, this type of dyslexic has given up on us all and gone away. One young boy I counselled could not even come out of his fantasy world during his counselling session. He just invited me in there – a world of knights, battles and kings where he was always the strongest and bravest. He was happier in there than in a world of people who had done nothing for him.

In the inner-defended group, I would also put those dyslexic children and adults who display all the symptoms of post-traumatic stress disorder (PTSD). These dyslexics are often sensitive and have been profoundly shocked by their first experience of school failure and bullying. They have never really recovered from this experience and present with all the classic PTSD symptoms of flashbacks, dreams (often of sharks or wolves), hypervigilance, exaggerated startle responses and avoidance of all situations that remind them of their first, damaging experiences. Sometimes – but not as often as common sense would dictate – they are school refusers and most are very troubled indeed. Some children with these severe symptoms cry constantly and are perpetually terrified of almost everything, night and day.

Other inner-defended children can show regressive symptoms and, in fact, the appearance of these symptoms suggests that the pressure of anxiety is becoming intolerable for them. These defences include sucking of fingers and clothing, bedwetting and soiling, rocking, holding of genitals, the constant company of furry toys. These are infantile and serious responses to stress, and we should all be aware that these are not vexatious behaviours but the symptoms of real distress.

My own view is that everyone – including children – can learn how to find coping strategies to comfort himself or herself when under stress, and dyslexic children and adults can be trusted to do so too. As observers, however, we have to notice when a coping strategy becomes a 'not coping' signal.

Low self-esteem

In research, dyslexic people are often found to have lower self-esteem than non-dyslexic controls. It is not surprising, therefore, that dyslexic people often present a counsellor with the task of 'improving' self-esteem.

I have to say that I find the notion of self-esteem to be a very slippery one. It is easy to acknowledge, hard to define and tricky to work with. My views are also complicated by the fact that self-esteem can have many different facets, including concepts of control, optimism, self-image, self-talk and internalised role models. Thus, which part of their self-esteem is 'low' for a particular client? Dyslexic children, for example, can have strikingly high ambitions for themselves alongside their literacy anxieties.

Importantly, aspects of 'low self-esteem' may have complicated pay-offs, which may be hard to extinguish without reframing whole life-systems including significant relationships. I have, for example, commonly encountered, among my more honest clients, acknowledgement that variants of the 'I'm so thin/fat/stupid/unattractive/poor me' dyslexic self-image can be used to charming and devastating effect with the opposite sex, or to annoy family members in satisfyingly passive/aggressive ways.

Also, the recently developed concept of 'post-traumatic growth' is based on research that shows that people who have had tough childhoods can become more creative and resilient adults than those with a more sheltered past. Some wonderful achievements have been made in spite of, or because of, challenging early experiences, and great endeavours can develop through compensation for inferiority feelings. Would Einstein, Steve Redgrave, Richard Branson or Eddie Izzard have achieved as much without the powerhouse of early dyslexic failure and disappointment? Linked to this, I am often startled at the wisdom, mature compassion and sensitive insights of dyslexic children, and the toughness, humour and kindness of dyslexic adults, all of which characteristics, I have no doubt, are forged in the furnace of their early experiences.

On the other hand, lack of self-esteem can lead to compensating actions of anger and crime (some studies show that over 50 per cent of inmates in British and American jails have severe literacy problems), as well as the pain and waste of human talent inherent in dyslexic breakdowns, depression, mental problems and suicide.

When I ask dyslexic clients how they would know that their self-esteem has improved, their answer usually revolves around reduced anxiety levels and a greater sense of control. Certainly, it is true that when dyslexic clients find some control over their anxiety through classic therapeutic process and/or the direct help of cognitive-behavioural techniques, it is this that makes them feel so much better generally.

It is absolutely essential to note, however, that many dyslexic people do not see improvements in their self-esteem arising from losing their dyslexia. It may seem an odd thing to say, but it is important to have respect for a dyslexic person's dyslexia. After all, their dyslexia is a significant part of who they are. Once we demonise their dyslexia, we demonise them. For example, I once did an exercise in guided imagery with a group of 10–13-year-old dyslexic girls and boys in which they were invited to exchange anything they owned for anything they wanted. It was an important learning moment for me when I found that only two in this group of over 30 children wanted to give up their dyslexia. If we respect dyslexia for what it is, and the advantages and experiences it can bestow, we are automatically respecting the dyslexic person just as they are. Being accepted for who we are is also an important component in good self-esteem.

I do have a suspicion that self-esteem is a dependent variable; that is, it co-varies in the presence of other primary variables. In other words, I do not think it is simply some ingredient that we can stockpile, but is something which arises naturally out of other things. Taking just one instance, there is a frequently documented rise in self-esteem when a dyslexic's reading and writing improve. Also, there is good evidence that the environment in which dyslexics find themselves can itself help. For example, an independent research study at East Court School, a specialist school for dyslexic children, found that measures of self-esteem among our children did not rise slowly in line with their time with us, but rose sharply on first entry then plateaued during their time with us. The primary variable was simply that these children no longer felt different, and were in an environment where they felt safe and valued.

A good relationship with significant others – whether a counsellor or some insightful and intuitive teachers – can also do a great deal to challenge the negative aspects of self-esteem and the destructive self-talk that goes with it. It is also helpful to encourage control and choice among dyslexics including the belief that if something is not working they can change it. They can do this by re-framing their attitude towards a situation or by focusing creatively on a solution rather than the rigidity of a problem.

The victim personality

A significant number of dyslexic people learn how to be victims from how other people have treated them. Being bullied and abused teaches victim behaviour in both obvious and subtle ways. Unfortunately, once this behaviour has been learnt, it can become quite useful. It can, for example, bestow power on a dyslexic person that may not have been achieved in other contexts. Being a victim can also enable a relationship with others where no other is on offer. It can produce a lot of attention, even though it may be negative attention. These are all seductive outcomes for a lonely and isolated person.

Some dyslexic people have acquired a victim personality, or have an entrenched attitude of 'learnt helplessness' – where they no longer believe that they have any control over their lives – which can persist through school, marriage, with their own partner and children, at work and in significant relationships for life.

In this role, they can invite other people – both children and adults – into a triangular relationship of 'persecutor' or 'rescuer' roles to their role as 'victim'. Anyone who accepts this invitation from the person in victim mode not only tacitly accepts the self-estimate of the person as victim but will also find themselves acting to support it.

With bullying, for example, while firm and immediate response can often quickly extinguish it, it is also the case that long-term bullying can have complex antecedents including the willing collusion of the victim. For example, if, despite all a school's best efforts, a dyslexic girl is somehow always being picked on, and her mother does not examine her daughter's role in these situations but responds habitually with protective, sympathetic attention, then she is providing fertile ground for victim behaviour to develop in her daughter. Teachers who find themselves tempted to rail against certain children whose behaviour is always somehow designed (which it is) to annoy them, need to be wary of what is going on, since it may be that they are being drawn into the persecutor role.

There is a payoff for the victim, in both these situations. Victim behaviour can draw attention away from failure. It can lead to increased attention from adults. By allowing all blame to reside in others, it can also remove the need to take personal responsibility for work and self.

It is also common to find that a particular manifestation of victim behaviour has happened before. For example, one dyslexic girl regularly saw me because all the other girls excluded her by 'ganging up on her'. I discovered that a similar pattern had occurred in all three of her previous schools, and with her sisters. Her parents, teachers, dinner ladies – a whole cohort – would comfort her. Digging more deeply, however, I found that she was constantly setting up irritating situations with other girls. This led to the desired effects – exclusion, victimisation, adult attention and excuses for work avoidance.

Much of this process is unconscious, but can be extremely powerful because the victim is getting a significant pay-off for this behaviour. If the other person also gets pay-offs for being a persecutor or rescuer because of their own psychology or background, then all parties collude with each other. What is interesting, in my experience, is how all the contributors to this beguiling but deeply toxic triangle manage to find each other.

Although a counsellor is trained how to respond to the victim role in clients, it requires vigilance to resist being sucked into rescuer or persecutor roles. I have counselled dyslexic children and adults who are deeply in victim roles and it is striking how strong the influence of this role can be. It is possible to feel intensely irritated by a child who has done no more than walk into the room, or be overwhelmed with a desire to give soothing, maternal protection to another who merely looks at you. Teachers and parents must also resist being drawn into these roles.

The other disturbing feature of this is that those locked in the triangle can move around its roles at will and in different contexts. Any adult, parent or professional can be a victim, persecutor or rescuer of a child, and any child can be a victim, persecutor or rescuer of a parent, professional or another child. The role permutations are frighteningly varied and prolific.

A useful strategy with all victim behaviour is to challenge it, gently, bring in it out into the fresh air – as long as this is done respectfully and does not become a subtle form of persecution. (Trust me, you do need to be on your toes.) Being open to the triangle and acting congruently, it is also possible to ease a child out of the victim role by encouraging them to examine and take responsibility for their role in any situation. I find that many dyslexic children and adults who are locked in the victim/learnt helplessness role are often a little churlish when it is examined. Nevertheless, they can then become quite fascinated as they gain insights into their own behaviour and see how such insights can give them control over their relationships with others and their place in the world.

There are other ways of resisting the self-estimate of learnt helplessness and victim personality. Speaking respectfully to someone in victim role, giving them choice, encouraging and believing in them, talking straight and being congruent (as outlined below) all play their part.

Nonetheless, outside of the counselling relationship, the most powerful contribution to extinguishing victim behaviour is simply success – any success. Improvements in literacy are very important, but any source of success – whether in sport, design, music – all play their part.

So often, success leads inexorably to confidence and the ability to take risks, particularly in how a dyslexic person negotiates the world. Foregoing familiar roles takes courage. Risk-taking and change take courage but success is seductive indeed. Only where other people have a stake in maintaining in a dyslexic a victim role (usually a family member) will it be chosen or preferred.

Relationships

If school is where dyslexic problems start, it is in relationships that the problems are perpetuated. Dyslexic low self-esteem springs directly from the attitudes and behaviour of other people. The many dyslexic people who reach the conclusion that they are worthless, 'rubbish', 'a pile of shit' (common descriptions) do so because they read this in the faces, voices, body language and direct statements of their parents, siblings, friends, peer group at school, teachers, relatives, work colleagues and employers. These people have also ridiculed and bullied dyslexic people on the basis of their poor reading, writing and spelling and all the times the dyslexic person is late, lost, disorganised, loses or forgets things, and misreads or misunderstands instructions. A dyslexic person has internalised this gale of critical information and often uses it to define both who they are and how they relate to other people. Not surprisingly, such experiences can contaminate the relationships that dyslexics have throughout their life. Dyslexic people can be suspicious, manipulative, withdrawn, defended and acutely sensitive to the smallest slight or perceived rejection.

Other relationship problems for dyslexics also start with the dishonesty and incongruence they experienced during their middle school years. Dyslexic children usually start their school life as trusting and optimistic as any child. After all, dyslexia itself is not a function of early psychological trauma, and the dyslexic child is no more likely to have early problems at school than any other child. Their dyslexia only becomes a problem when literacy difficulties emerge, and it is also at this time that important relationships acquire the incongruence that stokes so much latent anxiety in the dyslexic child. In short, everyone starts to treat the dyslexic child in a new and inexplicably uncomfortable way.

We are all defined largely through the behaviour and reactions of others, and this strange and incongruent behaviour lays the first germs of the stress and lack of confidence in self and others that mark out a life of relationships for dyslexic people. For example, when reading becomes a problem, dyslexic children cannot understand what is wrong. Working as hard as other children, they cannot fathom why they do not make progress. It is like slowly climbing a staircase in a dream. Yet, while they know that they are working, trying as hard as they can, they are told by adults, 'You're lazy. You're not trying. If only you would concentrate, work harder, do better, change.' So who is right?

Secondly, teachers and parents start looking at the dyslexic child, and start talking to them, in a new and worrying way. The dyslexic child senses that something is wrong, but no one will say what. To make matters worse, adults adopt these strange, bright smiles that seem, in some indefinable way, to say the opposite of what they mean. People are unnecessarily nice to you, and encouragement comes in odd, high voices. Parents say they are proud, happy, pleased, when the dyslexic child can clearly hear the undertone which says the absolute opposite; that they are disappointed, angry, frustrated. Then other children start to laugh at you. No one is straight with you any more. The person you really are starts to disappear as you try to become almost anyone in a frantic effort to please. Bewilderingly, all the huge effort you pour into work seems to be invisible to anyone but yourself.

My view is that the distrust of self, which is implicated in dyslexic low self-esteem and lack of confidence, starts from this early incongruence between what a dyslexic child knows and feels and what others tell him and how they react.

It is for this reason, I believe, that a route to helping a dyslexic to renegotiate his sense of self is through relationships with others that are both truthful and straight. I believe it is far worse to fudge the issue of dyslexia – 'Don't worry; it's fine' – than to be honest – 'OK, you're dyslexic. You'll have some problems. Let's look at how you can deal with them.'

I believe that this is why so many dyslexic children and adults feel significantly happier when they are diagnosed. Their problem is out in the open. Their perceptions and their feelings are finally proved right. With adults, the eventual diagnosis of dyslexia can do much to shift a lifetime – literally – of anguish. Now others can know, as they themselves have always known, that they are not stupid, lazy, spastic and all the other epithets thrown at them. It can feel triumphant. Suddenly their true self can be acknowledged.

In modelling a healthy relationship with any dyslexic, a good counsellor will make an outstanding contribution. They can do this by providing a different form of relationship based on therapeutic principles, or the 'core conditions', which include empathy, respect, congruence (or genuineness) and unconditional positive regard. The notion of 'core conditions' is one used in humanistic counselling and originated by Carl Rogers to describe the 'necessary and sufficient' conditions of a healing therapeutic relationship. I believe that these principles can also be used by anyone as a guide for a healthy relationship with both dyslexic children and adults. For example, respect and positive regard are implicit both in accepting dyslexic people as they are and by having good expectations of them. Many people have given up on dyslexics and take them at their own assessment – which is not always a positive one. Respect also implies high expectations. For example, I am clear that I do expect certain things from my dyslexic clients including self-responsibility, time-keeping and time boundaries within the session, and contracts of attendance and mutual behaviour, which we both agree. Such clarity of boundaries also provides a good model for how they can expect others to behave towards them.

Empathy expresses a deep understanding of the other person's position, and it can mean a lot to dyslexics to hear someone actually acknowledging what is difficult for them. For example, simply saying to a dyslexic child that you can see that they are finding something hard, or acknowledging how difficult and frightening it must be to forget things or get lost in large buildings, can be a really powerful stimulus by both relaxing and validating them. Congruence or genuineness as I have noted above, can make a dyslexic child or adult feel secure and respected and establish a trusting relationship.

I cannot overemphasise how much we also need to model new relationships for dyslexic people, particularly children, and show that we have boundaries, respect for ourselves as well as them, and can hear the truth, as well as be able to tell the truth to them. Above all, we should never, ever collude in any low self-image that dyslexic children or adults might have of themselves.

Some suggestions

1. All behaviour is a form of communication. All behaviour makes sense to the individual demonstrating it and has some positive intent for them. Rather than simply reacting to dyslexic behaviour, I invite you to read it. Useful questions are 'What is going on here?' 'What am I being invited to do?' 'What is the pay-off for this person in doing this?' 'What is powering this behaviour?' 'How can I offer a new, empowering agenda for this relationship?'
2. Sensitive adults can provide support for dyslexic children and adults by reminding them that they have choice and talent, and by challenging negative self-talk. There is a big difference between treating a dyslexic person as someone with a problem, or as someone with a problem they can deal with. Guilty, anxious mothers and kind but collusive teachers can disempower dyslexics. Such behaviour reinforces the dyslexic person's suspicion that they are useless. It says, 'You can't look after yourself. You are disabled. Give up '.
3. Trust your instincts. If a dyslexic person is seriously worrying you, then act on it. Changes in behaviour, self-harm, suicide threats, clear distress, withdrawal should all be addressed urgently and professional help sought. Having said that, helping and supporting dyslexics is not the same as counselling them, and this is best left to professionally trained and accredited counsellors and therapists. The most common problem with unofficial 'counselling' comes when the person being helped becomes over-attached, in the eyes of the helper, or starts to demonstrate dramatic, new and uncontained behaviours or extreme distress, including frightening memories. The helper then panics and abandons the person they are 'counselling' who may be dangerously vulnerable, leading to even more serious problems than presented originally.
4. Remember the positive. Dyslexic adults and children are not only talented but can be

really quite tough and enjoy challenges. After all, they have spent their lives surviving the most traumatic and discouraging circumstances, and have developed coping strategies of the most sophisticated and intelligent kind.

Nonetheless, for dyslexics to believe in themselves, we have to believe in them first. You can encourage self-belief in dyslexics simply because you believe in them. They can take personal responsibility because you believe they can.

Useful starting points are 'If it's not working, change it' and 'You'll only get the same outcome, if you use the same input. Change the input and see what happens.' The most powerful phrase of all can simply be 'I believe that you can do things differently.'

References and resources

Chapter 1

Chiat, S. (1979) 'The role of the word in phonological development', *Linguistics* **17**, 591–610.

Cooper, J. (1985) 'Children with specific learning difficulties: the role of the speech therapist', in Snowling, M. (ed.) *Children's Written Language Difficulties*. Windsor: NFER-Nelson.

Ehri, L. (1980) 'The development of orthographic images', in Frith, U. (ed.) *Cognitive Processes in Spelling*. London: Academic Press.

Ehri, L. (1991) 'The Development of Reading and Spelling in Children', in Snowling, M. J. and Thomson, M. E. (eds) *Dyslexia, Integrating Theory and Practice*. London: Whurr Publishers.

Ehri, L. (1992) 'Reconceptualizing the development of sight word reading and its relationship to recoding', in Gough, P. B., Ehri, L. C. and Trieman, R. (eds). *Reading Acquisition*, 107–43, Hillside, NJ: Lawrence Erlbaum Associates.

Fawcett, A. (ed.) (2001) *Dyslexia: Theory and Practice*. London: Whurr.

Frith, U. (1980) 'Unexpected spelling problems', in Frith, U. (ed.) *Cognitive Processes in Spelling*. London: Academic Press.

Frith, U. (1985) 'Beneath the surface of developmental dyslexia', in Marshall, J. C., Paterson, K. E. and Coltheart, M. (eds) *Surface Dyslexia in Adults and Children*. London: Routledge and Kegan Paul.

Given, B. and Reid, G. (1999) *Learning Styles: A guide for teachers and parents*. Lancashire: Red Rose Publications.

Grunwell, P. (1985) '*Phonological Assessment of Child Speech*. Windsor: NFER-Nelson.

Krupska, M. and Klein C. (1998) *Demystifying Dyslexia: raising awareness and developing support for dyslexic young people*. London: Language and Literacy Unit.

Lindsay, G. (2001) 'Identification and Intervention in the Primary School' in Fawcett, A. (ed.) *Dyslexia: Theory and Good Practice*. London, Whurr.

Lundberg, H. and Hoien, F. (2001)'Dyslexia and Phonology', in Fawcett, A. (ed.) *Dyslexia: Theory and Good Practice*, London.

Marsh, G., Freidman, M., Welch, V. and Desberg, P. (1980) 'The development of strategies in spelling', in Frith, U. (ed.) *Cognitive Processes in Spelling*. London: Academic Press.

Munro, J. (1998) 'Phonological and Phonemic Awareness: Their impact on learning to read prose and to spell', *Australian Journal of Learning Disabilities* **3** (2), 15–21.

Reid, G. (1998) *Dyslexia: A practitioner's manual*. Chichester: Wiley.

Samuels, S. J. (1999) 'Developing reading fluency in learning disabled students', in R. J. Sternberg and L. Spear-Swerling (eds) *Perspectives on Learning Disabilities: Biological, Cognitive, Contextual*. Bolder, CO: Westview Press.

Snowling, M. (1985) 'Assessing reading and spelling strategies', in Snowling, M. (ed.) *Children's Written Language Difficulties*. Windsor: NFER-Nelson.

Snowling, M. (2000): *Dyslexia: A Cognitive Developmental Perspective*. Second edition. Oxford: Blackwell.

Snowling, M. and Stackhouse, J. (1996) *Dyslexia Speech and Language: A Practitioner's Handbook*. London: Whurr Publishers.

Stackhouse, J. and Snowling, M. (1992) 'Barriers to literacy Development in two cases of developmental verbal dyspraxia', *Cognitive Neuropsychology* **9** (4), 273–99.
Stackhouse, J. and Wells, B. (1997) *Children's Speech and Literacy Difficulties: A Psycholinguistic Framework.* London: Whurr Publishers.
Thomson, M. E. (2001) *The Psychology of Dyslexia: A handbook for teachers.* London: Whurr Publishers.
Thomson, M. and Watkins, E. (1998) *Dyslexia: A Teaching Handbook.* Second edition. London: Whurr Publishers.
Vail, P. L. (1992) *Learning Styles – Food for thought and 130 practical tips for teachers* K–4. Rosemont, NJ: Modern Learning Press.

Chapter 2

Goswami, U. (2000) *INSET Lecture to East Court School.*
Snowling, M. J. (2000) *Dyslexia.* Oxford: Blackwell.
Thomson, M. E. (2001) *The Psychology of Dyslexia: A Handbook for Teachers.* London: Whurr.
Thomson, M. E. and Watkins, E. J. (1998) *Dyslexia: A Teaching Handbook.* (Second edition). London: Whurr.

Chapter 3

Chinn, S. and Ashcroft, R. (1993) *Mathematics for Dyslexics.* London: Whurr.
Henderson, A. (1998). *Maths for the Dyslexic.* London: David Fulton Publishers.
Joffe, L. (1983) *Mathematics and Dyslexia.* Ph.D Thesis, University of Aston.
Miles, T. and Miles, E. (eds) (2002) *Dyslexia and Mathematics.* London: Routledge Falmer.
Sharma, M. (1989) Math Notebook Vol. 7–8. Framingham, Massachusetts: Cambridge University Press.

Chapter 6

Bender, Dr. M. (1971) *Stopping Hyper-activity.* Baltimore, MD: O'Dell & Cook.
Dennison, P. and Dennison, G. (1994) *Brain Gym (Edu-Kinesthetics).* California: Venture.
Goddard, S. (1996) *A Teacher's Window Into the Child's Mind.* Eugene, OR: Fern Ridge Press.
Gordon, N. and McKinlay, I. (1980) *Helping Clumsy Children.* London: Churchill Livingstone.
Hunt, P. (ed.) (1997) *Praxis Makes Perfect II.* Hitchin: The Dyspraxia Foundation.
Portwood, M. (1999) *Developmental Dyspraxia* (2nd edn). London: David Fulton Publishers.
Portwood, M. (2000) *Understanding Developmental Dyspraxia.* London: David Fulton Publishers.

Index